Style Evolution

How to Create Ageless Personal Style
in Your 40s and Beyond

Kendall Farr

Illustrations by
Anja Kroencke

GOTHAM BOOKS

For my mother, Diony Stoddard Farr
my first and forever style inspiration

Published by Penguin Group (USA) Inc.
375 Hudson Street, New York, New York 10014, U.S.A.
Penguin Group (Canada), 90 Eglinton Avenue East, Suite 700, Toronto, Ontario M4P 2Y3,
Canada (a division of Pearson Penguin Canada Inc.); Penguin Books Ltd, 80 Strand, London
WC2R 0RL, England; Penguin Ireland, 25 St Stephen's Green, Dublin 2, Ireland (a division
of Penguin Books Ltd); Penguin Group (Australia), 250 Camberwell Road, Camberwell,
Victoria 3124, Australia (a division of Pearson Australia Group Pty Ltd); Penguin Books India
Pvt Ltd, 11 Community Centre, Panchsheel Park, New Delhi–110 017, India; Penguin Group
(NZ), 67 Apollo Drive, Rosedale, North Shore 0632, New Zealand (a division of Pearson
New Zealand Ltd); Penguin Books (South Africa) (Pty) Ltd, 24 Sturdee Avenue, Rosebank,
Johannesburg 2196, South Africa

Penguin Books Ltd, Registered Offices: 80 Strand, London WC2R 0RL, England

Published by Gotham Books, a member of Penguin Group (USA) Inc.

First printing, April 2009
10 9 8 7 6 5 4 3 2 1

LIBRARY OF CONGRESS CATALOGING-IN-PUBLICATION DATA
Farr, Kendall, 1959–
    Style evolution: how to create ageless personal style in your 40s and beyond /
Kendall Farr.
        p. cm.
    ISBN 978-1-592-40421-6 (hardcover)
    1. Women's clothing. 2. Fashion. 3. Middle-aged women. I. Title.
    TT507.F37 2009
    646.4'04—dc22   2008043376

Printed in the United States of America
Set in New Caledonia Family and Helvetica Neue Family
Designed by Susi Oberhelman

contents

introduction

What does it mean to have reached middle age in a time of celebrity adulation, youth obsession, stripper culture, and the Real Housewives franchise? For starters, it means you are likely to be confused and frustrated when you shop for new clothes—at a time when your personal style has never been more important. Dressing well and looking current and grown-up in middle age is not only a vital reflection of self-regard but of the attitude we wish to project to the world.

Let me share a story, A Tale of Two Middle-Aged Women and Their Jeans: Not long ago, my assistant and I watched two women ordering coffee at the bar of a fashionable French boîte in SoHo. The first woman was dressed in Levi's. They were simple, dark indigo, and the straight cut was neither loose nor tight and skimmed her curves in a flattering way. A white cotton shirt, sleeves rolled casually to her elbows (again, skimming), a colorful leather tote of no visible pedigree and flat sandals accented her look. Her collarbone-length hair was loose and unfussy and warm, natural-looking highlights framed her simple makeup. Most striking of all, she radiated a self-confidence that was irresistible. Her age was difficult to pin down. She might have been 40 or 55. It hardly mattered. "I want to be her when I grow up," said my 24-year-old assistant.

"She looks absolutely great," I added. "But yipes, look at *her*!"

A few feet away I'd clocked the backside of a woman in black, tourniquet-tight "premium denim." The matchstick cut, along with high platform pumps, gave her the requisite licorice stick legs-of-the-minute. The rhinestones on her back pockets drew my eye to a tortilla flat bum. A skin-tight, cap-sleeved T-shirt (revealing considerable bra bulge and dimpled upper arms) and an of-the-second bag with multiple zippers and charms hanging from the strap punctuated her look. Flat-ironed, platinum-blond hair reached the middle of her back with the help of obvious-looking extensions. When she turned to leave, coffee in hand, I saw she was at least 50 or perhaps a bit older. It wasn't her age that mattered but rather the way her "look" (the same "uniform" of many a millennial girl standing at the coffee bar, by the way) turned a floodlight on the very thing she was trying to hide. Her kohl-rimmed eyes and oversized glossy lips further exposed an age anxiety that was uncomfortable to watch.

Numerical age—particularly "middle age"—means less and less these days. One's sensibility is a far more relevant and meaningful term for defining a modern woman's fashion choices in her 40s, 50s, 60s, and beyond. The styles we chose in our 20s or 30s have (or should have) evolved as we matured. What all women of a certain age should now go for, I believe, is a wardrobe that is essentially ageless and timeless, that reflects being grown-up while it visually asserts self-confidence, individuality, and ease.

A woman's 20s are about style surfing, chasing trends for provocation and outrage, and for experimenting with as many personas as possible. Her 30s are for growing up and into her fashion identity along with developing an eye for silhouette and quality. Her 40s are a kind of staging decade for a new approach to her style that will wear well in the years ahead. Many women have an epiphany (or a full-blown crisis) when they recognize that styles they've worn since their 20s and 30s have run their course and simply don't look right anymore. If by 40 you find yourself asking, "How am I supposed to look now?" if you are unsure when shopping for new things or ambivalent about buying new clothes because you are stuck in a style rut, don't worry about it. It happens to almost every woman at this point in the journey (even fashion stylists). This is also a time of physical and mental transition for women and many complain that once they reach a certain age they feel invisible.

Your personal style is one important way to stay visible and relevant, yet you may start to hate shopping because so few clothes in your favorite stores seem designed with you in mind.

In every fashion season designers invoke many of the same tired muses: the ingenue, the schoolgirl (or schoolboy), the sexy secretary, the debutante, and the dissipated socialite. Gorgeous, malnourished teenagers wearing the world's most expensive clothes (many silly, frilly, and utterly out of touch with reality) are meant to fuel our middle-aged aspirational appetites. Designers know this works. While the desire for luxury goods is at a fever pitch, so is female body anxiety (the incidence of eating disorders among midlife women is on the rise).

If you've succumbed from time to time to the images in fashion magazines and celebrity rags, you are far from alone. Unless you live in the extreme remove of an ashram or a space pod, these images are unavoidable, they are everywhere, and no woman is entirely immune to them.

We are an unprecedented group, we baby boomers. While some of us were hippies and others of us were yuppies, we all share a rejection of traditional notions of middle age. That most of us don't dress like our mothers is well documented. That we dress to please ourselves is also well known by researchers. I read recently that to reach "us"—meaning to harness our staggering spending power—the approach should be "psycho-graphic" rather than demographic. Yet retailers struggle to pin down what we want because our psychology is represented variously in a female tribe with diverse notions of self-adornment, self-improvement, and what it means to dress appropriately for one's age.

You may well ask: "Exactly what does age-appropriate dressing mean anymore? I'm 50, but I feel 30 and I want to look young." This is an important question and one your stylist thinks about with every shopping trip for her advertising gigs, for her clients (those between 40 and 60), and for herself! Your stylist is also a woman of a certain age.

For the past several years, the design direction for affordable clothes has offered a few specific choices—none of them acceptable, in my opinion.

First, the '90s world of basics: a dreary landscape of unremarkable tees, twinsets, boxy jackets, bootcut stretch pants and washed denim jeans, A-line, pencil, or the token "flirty" bias-cut skirts. An "update" of these basics spawned something far worse: moderate and bridge lines trying to create "young" looks for midlife bodies by borrowing details from news-making lines like Marc by Marc Jacobs or Chloé, to absurd affect. The same matronly and boxy shapes were tarted-up with a row of Sgt. Pepper buttons here or a ruffle and a beaded appliqué there. Why? Because we brand-literate (and fed-up) over-40s had run screaming to the racks of the contemporary department looking for current styling and fit, novelty, and youthful details. We ended up with too many low-rise jeans, velour tracksuits, faux vintage, and baby-doll looks.

While there may no longer be any tried-and-true rules or prescriptions for dressing appropriately (at any age), for us there should be. Ladies, some stuff simply doesn't work anymore. There is a whole world of choice that exists between the blanched monotony of basics and the soft-porn style seen on *The Real Housewives of Orange County*.

Especially now, when you have never known more or had more personal gravitas, it is essential to cultivate a new perspective if you feel stuck. It's time to choose the clothes that will keep your look evolving in an inspiring and individualistic way. By 40, you have lived and learned, and the last thing you want to do is dress unremarkably or in styles so incongruously young that you appear to be at war with yourself.

There is *young* and there is *youthful*. And while youthful infuses a look with an ageless and timeless charm, verve, and a dose of nerve, young is where most middle-aged women run off the rails. And let's be frank, ladies, our culture assesses women—especially midlife women—by a brutal set of standards every day. While "mutton-dressed-as-lamb" is commonly lobbed at the woman faking it in a blouse-length dress from Forever 21, when was the last time you heard a 50ish man dressed in cargo shorts and a wallet chain from Abercrombie described as "beef-jerky-dressed-as-calf"? Exactly.

I am here to show you how your wardrobe can keep pace with the rest of your life. So before we begin our work together, I'll ask you to keep this in mind: This is not a revolution. There will be no waging war on your closet or your body. This is an evolution: a slow and steady way to intelligently reevaluate your style one piece at a time. Let's begin your *style evolution* . . .

1 your style

We've all heard style pronouncements such as 50 is the new 40 and 40 is the new 30. Accomplished, affluent, and fit, baby boomers and the front end of Gen X are more style conscious and brand literate with every passing fashion season. We also have modern science and an ever-greater menu of "cosmeceuticals" with which we can turn back the clock. Gone are the days when a woman must wear the look of each decade like rings in a tree trunk. But even with more information and more brands to choose from (and the experience and sophistication that comes with age), it can be very tricky to arrive at a modern look that achieves an aesthetic balance between Forever 21 and matronly jolie madame.

The fashion designer Michael Kors recently said, "No longer is there 'mutton-dressed-as-lamb.' " And it's true that we ladies can wear whatever we like—at any age—but should we? For now, here at the beginning of our stylist-client relationship, let's not worry about what looks too young or too old, and let's talk about a personal style that is ageless.

"Ageless" is first an organic, natural approach to fashion. It is based on wearing good design with the right foundations underneath— it is a given that creating a flattering silhouette on a body (at any size) is appealing (at any age).

How would your stylist describe a woman with ageless personal style? She's the savvy woman who:

- Understands that the softer a woman's body becomes, the more structure she needs in her clothes.
- Bypasses gimmicks, detail overload, and tricky shapes— all of which can look very aging on midlife ladies.
- Keeps up with trends and knows exactly what she's looking for. She has a trained eye for the smart

interpretation rather than anything that looks like it belongs in the junior department.

- Knows that details like buttons or prints that would look adorable in a child's size, when if made to fit her, make her look matronly and out of touch.
- Creates a canvas with her clothes and wears a mix of current and distinctive accessories—new and old—to express her singular style.
- Achieves a look that is unstudied and seemingly effortless (which she understands is complete hooey, as it takes paying attention to style and making an effort in order to look good).

Notice her mixing seamlessly with her younger colleagues, on the street, in her workplace, traveling, or on a date: A woman with ageless style looks individual and plugged-in to what is current, but she interprets things her own way. She has achieved a visual balance between the youthful age in her head and the age on her passport (no one else's business, I might add).

Not for nothing do both women in their 60s and women in their 20s wear (and covet) many of the same pieces from Lanvin, Yves St. Laurent, Chanel, Oscar de la Renta, Carolina Herrera, Prada, Marni, and Dries Van Noten—all examples of intelligent design that reexamines classics—clothes that are in touch with modern women's lives (if not their wallets).

Years ago, Christian Dior said that "there are two stages in a woman's life: girlhood and womanhood." A clear-cut style prescription for postwar times, "womanhood" was the time to be dressed in refined tailoring, to display polish and glamour. A woman with a hint of "girlhood" in her outfit was considered in bad taste. Period. In the twenty-first century these definitions aren't as clear cut. While advertising images promote the look of extreme youth, many designers follow suit with clothes designed for a kind of extended "girlhood."

Once we are into our 40s most of us have had one fashion decade during which we developed a few uniforms that we felt good wearing. Most of us refer to our proven winners when choosing updates of our favorite things. Many of us cling resolutely, like a life raft, to the very same things year after year. The fact is, by doing this we can get stuck in a rut, the result being that we look out of date or out of touch with the times. It is at this point in our lives that we need to reevaluate what is working for us and what isn't. There comes a time when a woman's style needs to catch up with the rest of her life.

Here are a few style profiles that show how we can fall into a style rut. See if you identify with any of them. They describe your stylist's faithful observations of women over 40 in New York City and all over the country. I've seen versions of these profiles in the U.K., in Europe, and even recently in South America and Latin America. You may find elements of your own style in (at least) one of these:

Matched: Most comfortable when she finds pieces that go together in outfits. If she can find it all from one designer, department, or catalogue, better yet. Whether high fashion and chapter-and-verse from a designer's look-book, or hypercoordinated from a store/catalogue, she allows for few variations and thus little margin for error.

Midcentury Matron: A style informed by Jackie Kennedy during her White House years and the late '50s—American classics her mom wore. Her college style would be described as preppy. Blazers. Oxford-cloth shirts. Khakis. She loves the same shifts and clam diggers in "fun" prints she wore then. Favors grosgrain bows and eyelet trims on clothes, shoes, and bags. Bright-colored cable knits, twinsets, and madras and tartan plaids remain wardrobe staples. Let's not forget to mention the tidy strand of pearls.

Middlescent: The "Peer Mom" who swaps super-skinny jeans with her teenager. Shops for trendy pieces for her daughter—and herself—from Forever 21, BCBGirls, Juicy Couture, Abercrombie, and Victoria's Secret Pink, including cropped polos, thermal henleys, and low-rise yoga pants. Wears Ugg boots, flip-flops, and sparkly ballet flats. Delighted to point out that she and her daughter wear all the same stuff.

The Girly Girl: Peer Mom's fashion-savvy friend; she shops the contemporary department for sweet '60s- and '70s-inspired pieces by Anna Sui, Nanette Lepore, and Marc by Marc Jacobs. Midthigh-length dresses, bright-colored tights, and chunky platform shoes are all favorites. Loves little lacy trims, embroidery, and shrunken versions of retro "lady suits."

Novelty and Status Addict: Whether wait-listed at YSL or guest-designed at Target, she wants it. She canvasses fashion magazines, the tabloid weeklies, Style.com, and blogs like BagSnob.com for editor's picks, what celebrities are wearing this week, and whatever has been ordained as "New and Now" by the fashion press. Wears the most recognizable runway pieces. Never read the memo about the demise of the It Bag. Has been known to carry a Birkin and a Goyard tote together. If an actress whose look she admires promotes a brand, this validates her choice.

Overripe: She is a toned and fit 50-something, and to be certain you notice she'll serve up a short skirt (she has great legs, after all) and a low-cut top with a side order of cleavage. Tight, body-conscious clothes have always worked for her and she'll wear them until . . . who knows when?

That Nineties Uniform: Somewhere between the '80s "power dressing" of her early career and fashion's millennial shift to the girl-ish woman dressed in sheer chiffon and baby-doll dresses, she adopted an utterly practical '90s wardrobe. Black jackets and black pants fill her closet. Maybe some "natural" colors like mauve or mint green to wear with her khakis. White shirts. Crew-neck sweaters worn over crew-neck T-shirts, under blazers. Can't live without stretch bootcut pants in . . . black. Nondescript nylon backpacks and tote bags and low, square heels are her accessories.

Active Wear(er): Can't remember the last time she bought "clothes." Lives in fleece jackets and vests, T-shirts and sweatpants. Loves comfort (to hell with fashion) as much as she loves her Crocs, clogs, and aerobic shoes. To dress up for a night out, she'll wear a black velour hoody with her jeans.

If you find yourself stuck in any of these profiles, consider the following DIAGNOSES and SOLUTIONS. Even if you don't recognize your style in some of them, be sure to read through each of the Solutions, as most of this advice is applicable to all of us. When something is universally applicable, it will be identified as ADVICE FOR ALL. Now let's look at our style profiles with an eye to style evolution.

matched

DIAGNOSIS: Time for a less rigid prescription for shopping. Pre-coordinated outfits never include the most essential ingredient of personal style: the personal part.

SOLUTION: First, a reminder: Fashion cycles are also color cycles. Trends forecasters and color experts are paid millions to predict what shapes and colors women will want to wear in the next year. Designers

and manufacturers buy a lot of the same information, and that's why you can walk across a retail floor
filled with racks of similar colors and patterns. It's
also why you'll see pieces and colors at Neiman
Marcus and at Target that are similar. This
is actually good news for you. You can
pick and choose individual pieces that
are compatible—not precoordinated—in
various price ranges. When you shop from
a high-fashion collection, often the palette is
very specific. The colors and prints have been
developed to look unique, and thus it makes sense to
buy a few things that work together. Buying from just
about anywhere else, I'll hasten to add, means that
you can mix and match easily.

ADVICE FOR ALL: Whenever you feel like the
shopper's equivalent of a deer caught in headlights:

▶ **Choose a palette:** Failsafe—black, white,
navy, and khaki. Good in cities. Good in sub-
urbs. Good at resorts. I am an advocate of
having a good-quality neutral (black or white)
pantsuit in your wardrobe, so choose a jacket and pants together.
When you are wearing a suit, the pieces should be from the same
fabric and the same dye lot.

▶ **Build a foundation:** Jackets, lightweight knits, trousers, and skirts
in both refined and casual fabrics. Include dark blue and white
denim jeans in the lineup. These are indispensable pieces—the
backbone of your wardrobe—and they should be the very best
quality you can afford. If need be, buy less and buy better (one
of your stylist's constant refrains). Look for current silhouettes,
lengths, sleeve treatments—all in shapes that flatter your shape.
As you gain confidence going it on your own, add in some skin-
flattering richer tones and bright colors to build on a wardrobe that
mixes old favorites with new pieces.

▶ **Fight your old habits:** Pulling together your own look can be this
simple: Wear black, white, navy, or neutral tones on your bottom and
neutral or color for your top combined with tonal accessories. Simple
and graphic. Avoid the reflex to buy everything from one place.

▶ **Mixing prints and patterns (on your own):** Prints, stripes, plaids, and tweeds all add personality and breadth to the mix. Patterns of two, three, or many colors will have a dominant color, a secondary color, and one or more splashes of accent color in the pattern. In a successful mix of pattern and texture the dominant color should be clearly visible in each pattern. If you have to squint to find the common color in one of the pieces, you may end up with a combination that looks jangly. A secondary color that appears clearly in each pattern helps the look gel.

midcentury matron

DIAGNOSIS: Many of the traditional pieces that the MCM wears are classics that represent a blue-chip standard of their kind. Trouble is, our preppy's tried-and-true looks have been hijacked by countless designers and run through the irony mill. While *les jeunes filles* can wear the latest cheeky riff in the Preppy Handbook and look charming, on a 40-something woman the effect is often frumpy.

SOLUTIONS: No seismic shifts required in your wardrobe but let's start by looking beyond "old guard" brands and specialty stores for some current shapes:

▶ **Remixes:** Designers and manufacturers won't abandon their seasonal takes on classic shapes anytime in the foreseeable future. Take stock of the pieces you feel best in and wear most often. You will find that the old-school pieces you wear have all been nudged along by trends. If the fit is flattering and looks up-to-date, you will look up-to-date. Drape and a skimming fit should replace boxy. For every traditional blazer, barn jacket, pair of khakis, or bright knit sweater, there exists a parallel retail universe of newer takes on the very same things.

▶ **Details, details:** An updated choice of fabrics, textures, colors, and prints can change the landscape in your closet. Instead of another classic navy flannel blazer, try on a few shaped jackets in rich colors and neutrals in wool or cotton tweed or bouclé. Colorful prints can look dynamic or witty, or they can look like children's wear. Rather than clubby flowers, pink elephants, or waterfowl, try on an abstract floral, geometric, or scarf print. Think more Pucci than Lilly Pulitzer.

middlescent

DIAGNOSIS: The Cool Mom, the Teenile Mom, the MILF are all running gags about the middle-aged woman dressed in clothes made for girls in their teens and 20s. Wearing young gear will not make you look younger. On the plus side, your style is casual and unfussy, but it is time to elevate your look with items of better quality, with more coverage and more sophisticated details. And no, nothing will look like the "Mom clothes" of your worst nightmares.

SOLUTIONS: First, let's make a brief inventory of the "young" fashion that should be removed from your closet and from future shopping lists:

▶ **Skinny jeans and low, low-rise (hip-bones or below):** Time for a higher rise, a contoured waist, and no more rear-view exposure. While we are on the subject, no more whiskering, faux-distress (rips and fraying), dirty denim, or very light blue washes.

▶ **Very short skirts:** Lengths three inches above the knee are as short as a middle-aged woman (even with truly great legs) should go.

▶ **A cropped anything** that reveals skin.

▶ **Slogan, cartoon, or logo tees** (don't care who has them in their current collections).

▶ **Embellishment overload:** Sparkles, glitter, embroidery on jean legs and pockets, and any other "bedazzled" items (especially all together).

- **Young, generic footwear:** Chuck the UGGs. No more wearing rubber flip-flops everywhere (except at the beach, a spa, or at home).
- **"Young" jewelry:** Stacks of cheap bangle bracelets, lots of thread-thin chains with charms, hoop earrings with charms, rawhide necklaces or bracelets, especially with charms. No more trips to Claire's and Forever 21.
- **No bra straps showing** and no more black or colored bras visible under tanks and camisoles.

ADVICE FOR ALL: Take inventory of your favorites:

- **Jeans:** Instead of another super-low-rise pair, try on pairs from the new breed of denim designers who cut higher rises, contoured waists (which sit slightly higher in the back than in the front), and a smashing fit for your bottom. Try on a pair with a trouser cut as well. Choose the darkest indigo and bootcut or straight legs. We'll talk more about fit and brands later.
- **Jackets:** Do a little research at the top—the designer floor. Start just with tailored jackets. It doesn't matter if the prices are too high (of course they're too high!). Take in the shapes, colors, and fabrics and the overall look of what is current from line to line. Try on what you like and make a note of how the shoulders fit and where the hem rests on your hips. This is the best way to later find the look at a more comfortable price. Every woman should have at least one jacket with a flawless fit and that lengthens her body line. Jeans and a well-cut jacket is a combination that leads the charge for ageless style.

the girly girl

DIAGNOSIS: It's fine to wear a trend, but it should never be literal. Retro-redux is designed for girls in their 20s who can pull off the irony and the look of kindertart that shows up in a lot of this stuff. In the plus column, you feel best in feminine clothes. It's time to raise the womanhood and sophistication quotient in your wardrobe.

SOLUTIONS:

▶ **Less will be more:** In the same department and from the very same contemporary designers you favor you can get lucky from time to time. Knowing what to look for first requires research at the top. Walk the designer floor and notice the color palette: darker, richer, muted, maybe offbeat bright colors. Details are used in a sparing and focused manner. No little lace edges, eyelets, cheap-looking gemstones, beads, and embroidery, which are often gobbed on to contemporary pieces to tart things up for young women who want to look a lot more cheeky than chic.

▶ **Change your palette:** Look for black, navy, white, ivory, vegetable dye colors, very muted metallics—in appropriations of the pieces you've seen in the designer department for much, much more. This is a strategy for a more subtle and grown-up look.

▶ **Longer lengths:** Time to lengthen those hems to knee length or just above. No more midthigh minis—it's time to start a (gradual, if you must) withdrawal. You will have an easier time getting the right look by shopping the lines considered contemporary bridge.

novelty and status addict

DIAGNOSIS: NSA will never have a problem looking part of a season. She keeps up with what is current in any trends cycle and then some. However, few things telegraph age anxiety like a slavish attention to ad campaigns and must-have looks. Teens and 20-somethings are expected to ride any bandwagon as they thrash out an individual style of their own. Middle-aged women need to craft a style that is more personal and less about designers' sensibilities.

SOLUTION: Step away from the "Big Looks" and go easy on the "It" accessories at any price.

ADVICE FOR ALL:

▶ **Variation:** There will always be variations on a theme—a series of "exits," as you have undoubtedly noticed if you look at Style.com or Elle.com—within any collection. The ageless approach is to wear current but less recognizable pieces. Go for similar pieces that you can easily mix with what you own and from other designers, from stores and prices high to low.

overripe

DIAGNOSIS: When a middle-aged woman displays lots of cleavage, legs, or booty in public she reveals more than just her "assets." She risks exposing insecurities about her sex appeal, that while natural for any woman, are better not put on display. It also lacks the sense of subtlety that is very attractive to men as well as other women. While your stylist will tell you that she is very impressed that you still fit into those tight and short Léger and Alaïa bandage dresses from the early '90s, perhaps it is time to cultivate a look with a little more mystery.

SOLUTIONS: A velvet hammer rather than a sledge hammer is more seductive—at any age. Choose one focal point:

▶ **Your top:** When a dress is long, a skirt is full, or you are wearing pants (with a fluid skimming drape), create a focal point with your neckline and your arms. Halter, strapless, and portrait necklines are flattering options providing your skin looks smooth and toned. If not—no big deal—just choose what will smooth over any obvious (and natural) signs of aging. A low-cut bustier top revealing lots of skin and cleavage (yes, even under a jacket) with pants will look pushed up and past its prime. Any dress bodice or top low enough to rest just above your nipples or bra edge, or that plunges to your waist does not leave nearly enough to the imagination.

▶ **Your bottom:** Shorter lengths create a spotlight for your legs, so balance the view with a more covered top.

▶ **Shoulder styles:** Wide necklines revealing bared shoulders; low backs that drape and cowl.

▶ **Ease the fit:** Pieces that skim your curves will look plenty seductive and more attractive than the extreme look of anything skintight. We will talk later about the designers who can be relied upon for subtly sexy pieces.

that nineties uniform

DIAGNOSIS: In the plus column: You have reliable, indispensable foundation pieces to build upon as you expand your wardrobe. Your clothing should reflect more of you than your preference for buying multiples of the same things. If looking beyond a stack of merino V-necks seems overwhelming, don't get frustrated. Adding breadth and individuality to your wardrobe is not hard if you begin the process like this.

SOLUTION: Do some pruning—a periodic closet sweep is an essential part of maintaining a wardrobe that looks up to date. Trim your collections of like items and hang on to only the very best quality neutral, infinitely mixable pieces in each category. Thin out the color scheme as well. Again, keep only the best-quality classic but current-looking jackets, coats, and tops that flatter your skin tone.

ADVICE FOR ALL:

▶ **Shoes:** You should have up-to-date toes and heels (at any height). Nothing says "out of it" like wearing shoes—especially new shoes— that have a dated look.

▶ **Handbags:** It is a huge (growing every month, it seems) and cultish world of bags out there. Don't be thrown by the vast selection in most stores or online, as most of it is overdesigned and really young. Streamline your search and look for an uncomplicated shape. Commit to buying a new one in the best leather you can afford. Choose spare details. The more buckles, straps, grommets, studs, mixed materials, or a feverish combination of all of the above, the less sophisticated-looking the bag. You don't have to confine yourself to black or brown leather either. Choose a color—red, plum, a gray-blue, or a shade of green, for example, to elevate anything you wear, from jeans to dresses.

▶ **Accessories:** Jewelry, scarves, belts, and eyewear are all vital accents that should be updated periodically to look as current as your new clothes. Notice I did not say trendy. Eccentric, bold, personal—new and old—your accessories are the surest way to exert a presence and to add a measure of your personality to any outfit. Your choices should be in step with your new clothes, shoes, and bag(s). Nothing will sink your new "now" look faster than pieces that are nondescript or dated.

active wear(er)

DIAGNOSIS: While living in sweats and old jeans may fit your lifestyle, perhaps it's become easier to reject fashion rather than face the anxiety (and intimidation) of looking for new clothes. It is a common dilemma. But here's the reality: To mix comfortably in a world as rabidly visual and looksist as ours has become, you'll need to expand your repertoire. Not insurmountable. It can be simple, but you do need a system.

SOLUTIONS: Don't shop for items all at once:

▶ **Take time to think about a few things:** Make a list of what you do most, where you go, and what's missing in your closet. This is the first step to creating a more versatile wardrobe.

▶ **Simplify your search:** Start by adding a well-cut jacket, a lightweight, goes-everywhere car or trench coat in a flattering and modern-looking fabric, and a few pairs of jeans with a current-looking fit. Bootcut or skimming straight legs in dark indigo wash. No elastic waists, pleated waistbands, or full legs with tapered ankles. These are universally unflattering—on any body. There are more modern-looking options out there that will provide the right fit.

▶ **Keep only the flattering stuff:** Weed out the overwashed, oversized, pilling, or otherwise sprung pieces. Keep only what looks current and has a skimming, streamlined look.

▶ **Layer with your sport tops:** A lightweight, zip-front jacket or vest, for example, can look great as a liner and layering piece under a jacket or coat in a refined fabric. One of the many ways to achieve a mix of high and low.

▶ **Look for double agents:** Pieces with a crossover appeal—both for work and that can mix fluidly with the rest of your wardrobe. Sport shapes like windbreakers, zip-front vests, motocross jackets, peacoats that are cut in high-quality ready-to-wear fabrics, e.g., wool, cashmere, sweater knits, satin, cotton sateen, as well as tech-nylons, leather, and suede. Since seasonal research always begins at the top, pay attention to the way many designer collections include sport shapes in luxe-looking, unexpected fabrics.

A FEW MORE THOUGHTS BEFORE WE MOVE ON. The pleasure you feel in wearing certain colors, fabrics, textures, and shapes should guide, to some degree, your choice of new clothes. This adds the "personal" to personal style. But in order to reframe your perspective about your body in clothes, to leave behind a reliance on any out-of-date ideas (what looks old or young, right or wrong), you must rely on yourself to make a visual leap to a style, again, which is timeless: modern, current, plugged-in, effortless-looking, expressive, eccentric. Combine this mini-glossary with fashion's fundamentals: silhouette, line, balance, good-quality fabrics that drape on your body. Shake and pour: This blended "cocktail" is the recipe for ageless style. This may sound like a lot of ingredients, but as we move through each chapter you will find that they are all quite naturally connected.

2 dressing your body now

When I look at a woman of any shape or size—especially one over 40—whose clothes fit her badly, my first impression is that she's "standing five feet away from herself," to paraphrase the writer Henry James. No woman should wear clothes that don't fit. But it happens. At some point many of us simply stop looking closely enough at ourselves dressed. We are too busy dissecting ourselves while undressed. What woman in midlife doesn't have a laundry list of the body parts she'd gladly change? Yes, we ladies of a certain age will naturally fixate on the changing landscape of our undressed bodies and the particular effects of gravity and hormones on our various bits: the décolletage drifting south; the rib cage and hips that widened during pregnancy and stayed that way; the rounded "menopot" that defies Pilates and gym equipment and makes pants fit tricky; a fuller bottom; a flat bottom; a softening shoulder line; jiggly underarms; the armpit fold that hangs over the top of a strapless dress; that fleshy ripple above the elbow; and those inexplicable weight shifts that clearly have some estrogen-fueled mandate of their own. If you now feel like your body has a mind of its own, all the more reason to assert control over the fit of your clothes.

Lots of us rely on a mental picture of what good fit looked like years before. But dressing for a past body, or lamenting your changing body, or mentally Photoshopping your head onto an idealized body as you try on clothes is an exercise in frustration and delusion.

I'll share an observation with you: A few years ago, as I shopped for a project at Gucci, I noticed a woman wading from the dressing room in a very long, very slinky, and apparently weighty liquid gold jersey dress. In one hand she clutched yards of fabric, and in the other the glossy photo book of Gucci's current runway looks. Naturally, this was opened to the page featuring the same dress. Unremarkably, the model that wore this creation on the runway was a six-footer. On her, the dress looked like molten metal pouring down the length of her body. On the 50ish and five-foot-five (max) woman with the garden-variety bumps and rolls of midlife on display, the clingy dress didn't create quite the same effect. While one salesperson was dispatched to retrieve the highest heels in the shoe department, the store's crack seamstress calculated how to recut the dress to make it work. With tape measure, pins and chalk flying, seams were raised here and let out there while more than a yard of fabric was pinned up at the hem. Standing in a three-way mirror, I noticed that the woman had placed the runway photo of "The Dress" on the floor next to her. As she looked from the picture in the book to herself in the mirror, back to the picture and then to her image in the glass, I thought to myself, "There is no way she is leaving this store without some version of that dress." Her apparent determination to transform herself into the image in her head was fearsome to watch. Less surprising: the conviction of the staff to close the sale despite the fact that this alterations overhaul was a car wreck on her body. Not their problem. Indeed.

Embracing the "now" of your body—objectively considering every inch of it—and dressing it well is an unspoken statement that a woman knows and likes herself—NOW. Taking pride and pleasure in her midlife appearance—at any shape or size—should be as reflexive as breathing for every woman. Unhappily, it's not, and let's face it: Few fashion images in our culture encourage us to feel this way. So let's talk more about the visual power of the right clothes to erase pounds, "parts," and years, and you'll see a plan for your future wardrobe taking shape.

Shape, Drape, and Line

The unassailable trinity of good fashion design. Be uncompromising about the presence of these qualities in your clothes and you'll see an immediate improvement in your appearance. Anywhere you want to deemphasize is a place for pieces with clean and skimming shape and spare details. Anywhere you want the eye to linger is a place for details, a clever use of color or embellishment.

Your stylist advocates an organic solution of evolving your fit incrementally and regularly. The right shapes combined with great tailoring will make you appear leaner, lighter, longer. I cannot empha-size this enough. I am always gobsmacked when I see women wearing good clothes that fit badly. Too many women that I interviewed about their midlife bodies for this book complained to me that tailoring is a bother, that it's too expensive. Ladies, it is this simple for all of us: Avoid bad fit. Good fit is the equivalent of six months in the gym.

Here's something important to consider: Most affordable clothing is spatially flat—consisting of a front and a back. You, dear client, are far more than a front and a back, so always consider the 360-degree circularity of your body in clothes. What you wear must check out from every angle. Unless you happen upon a piece that is constructed of panels, gores, and well-placed seams that create a certain shape, it is vital to install needed shape with a few nips and tucks (from a tailor).

Stylists and tailors understand the power of choosing certain shapes, proportions, and constructions to manipulate the appearance of any silhouette. And when you have finished this chapter, you will too.

your stylist's upper body checklist

Choose a good frame. Always create a frame for your face: In a picture, any point where line and fabric meet bare skin is referred to as negative space. When I am styling an ad for a beauty product, for example, I choose tops with flattering and uncomplicated necklines to encourage the eye to look upward to the beautiful face wearing the foundation, cream, or lipstick. Think about the necklines you wear in the same way.

If you have a short or full neck, look for tops that create a low or deep vertical line with a V-neck or a U-neck top and necklaces with a bit of length to reinforce the up and down sweep of the eye.

If you have extensive sun damage on your chest, raise your neckline and the focal point. Choose one with a sweep of diagonally draped fabric that creates an attractive line across your shoulders and collarbone, or try a simple but elegant bateau neck. The eternal brilliance of the turtleneck is the option to cover the neck altogether, with a skin-flattering color; the drama of black (if it suits you flush to your face) or the right shade of white to draw the eye directly to your face. A baggy neckline will make you appear bigger.

Wear a truly great-fitting jacket

Numero Uno. A jacket that fits well defines the upper body and is the most essential wardrobe miracle worker for women of every shape and size. Pay attention to these critical fit details when you try on a new jacket or are debating whether to keep or toss an old favorite:

▶ **Shoulder line:** The definition (or lack of it) of a jacket's shape begins here. The line should meet the edge of your shoulders. If the line falls below your natural shoulder line, you will appear larger.

▶ **Mind the sleeves:** Pay attention to the cut of the armhole as well. When an armhole is cut high and the sleeves just skim the upper arm, it creates a vertical line from your shoulder to jacket hem. Skimming is always slimming and lengthening. Whether big around the armholes with wide sleeves or tight across the shoulder, armholes, and sleeves, the visual effect is fattening.

▶ **Check the sleeves:** Whether long to the wrist or cropped at midarm or elbow, they should taper in just slightly—which makes the arm appear thinner and longer. If they don't, have a tailor nip them in a bit.

▶ **Check the stance:** A tailoring term for the meeting point of lapel and buttons. How long is the V-line?

- **One-button:** Creates an elongated vertical line; the deep V-front slims the waist; fudges a more angular appearance. If you are full of bosom, choose a style that buttons just below your bust to avoid pulling and gapping.

- **Two-button:** Disguises a little padding between your bra and navel. There is no better article of clothing for disguising a full midriff and tummy. This is the most universally flattering jacket style for all shapes and sizes.

tip   As all things vertical are our friends, don't forget to try chalk stripes.

- **Three- and Four-buttons:** Shorter women and petites appear taller if the jacket stance is higher. The top button is best hitting midchest. Styles with a slight peplum or A-line fake a curvier silhouette for straight middles and hips.

And while we're talking about it: Oversized buttons are visually fattening. Big and colorful, multicolor combinations, big and shiny metal (ooh! especially shiny) will all draw the eye to big and round surfaces on your chest, torso, and hip. The quick take: You are big and round. Smaller and matte buttons are a better way to go. If you own or find a jacket you love with compact-mirror-sized buttons, change them—providing your tailor can reduce the size of the buttonholes without obvious stitches—and go for expensive-looking and subtle. Look for vintage or antique buttons. Nothing finesses inexpensive fabric like expensive-looking buttons. Your stylist once swapped too-large, too-shiny buttons on a black peacoat from Zara for some antique British navy buttons unearthed at a flea market. Voilà, the illusion of a much more expensive jacket!

▶ **A nipped waist:** However subtle, a nipped waist is an essential bit of installed shape for all of us. Vertical seams and diagonally placed slash pockets are features that reinforce a slimming line. If extra jacket fabric above your waist is a chronic condition, then most likely you have a short waist. Have your jackets tailored and try petites or petites-plus jackets.

▶ **Length:** Here you'll cross-reference with your edited shopping list (found in Chapter 3), of course, but a universally flattering length hits at high hip.

▶ **Reminder:** Avoid any hem that ends at the low hip or just above (where hips and bottom meet), as drawing a line across this point of your body will always create a fattening line.

▶ **Check your rear view:** Here is what you never want to see—two half-moons hanging below your jacket hem. When you do—even if you love the look of the jacket from the front—put it back. Try a jacket that hits the high hip and exposes enough of your backside (wearing the right underpinnings and choice of a bottom) to look proportionately curvy. Or opt for a jacket that skims the bottom of your bum for an elongating line. Always examine jacket fit in a three-way mirror to assure a flattering line from every angle.

▶ **Pocket placement:** Important. Big square patch pockets create a focal point wherever they are placed. Rectangular flaps placed at breast or hip level become focal points. Colorful contrast stitching or piping around a pocket is a guaranteed eyebeam. All of these treatments create a series of distracting horizontals, and as we know, horizontal is fattening. Look for pockets placed on the diagonal instead.

Wear truly great-fitting, crisp cotton shirts

Bra lines, fleshy or untoned upper arms, a full midriff are instantly smoothed over when you swap any clingy top for a skimming button-front shirt. Crisp fabric is anti-droop and visually uplifting. Open your collar and unbutton low enough to create a deep V-line that draws the eye upward and away from your middle. When your stylist is feeling a tad chunky, it's a steady diet of crisp white shirts, great accessories, and salads.

▶ Look for shaped vertical seams, darts, or side panels to avoid a square line.

▶ Whether princess or a treatment like corset (small raised seams from bust to waist sewn around the circumference of the shirt), look for shape in the construction. Always size up to accommodate a full bust. Have a tailor trim a little from the sides for a gap-free front.

▶ Long sleeves should hit at your wristbone. Personally, I love the look of an exaggerated French cuff, hanging well below my jacket cuff, and if you have long arms and are midheight to tall, give it a try. However, the correct measurement for conservative dress is half an inch to three quarters of an inch below a jacket's cuff.

Rethink your T-shirt fit

T-shirts are indispensable wardrobe staples. But for most of us the day arrives when our tried-and-true tissue weights or lightweight Lycra knits (especially in light colors) look fattening. It may be the upper arms that look too big for short sleeves; or bend over and it's the jelly-roll under your bra band; or sit down and it's cascading crullers above your navel. Skimming fit is always our objective, so go for T-shirts in midweight cotton jersey. To smooth over a bra bulge or midriff rolls, try one of the latest generation of nude tanks and tees with laser-cut edges that provide a line-free appearance under tees, shirts, and knits.

▶ **Large breasts:** T-shirt fit is as revealing as it gets. Reminder: Be certain the bra or bra cup camisole you choose gives you a line-free look from 360 degrees. Smooth cups and an underwire are essential for the lift and symmetry you need. Your torso will appear thinner with the right engineering.

▶ **Small breasts:** To increase the volume of your bustline, create lift and natural-looking symmetry with a smooth cupped bra or bra-cup camisole with an underwire. Try a style with a bump pad or add your own silicone gel pads placed where you need to fill things up—bottom or sides.

Try one of these lightweight gems under your favorite T-shirts and lightweight knits for smooth-looking coverage:

- **Avenue:** Seamless Shaping Tank—to size 24 DDD.
- **Cass & Co.:** Invisibellas V-neck tank; M/L, L/XL.
- **Cass & Co.:** Invisibellas three-quarter sleeve scoop neck—S/M, M/L, L/XL—for torso and upper-arm slimming.
- **Commando:** Tank TNK.
- **Flexees:** Everyday Control Camisole (available with or without a bra cup).
- **Sassybax:** Torso Trim and Torso Trim with Underwire—S–1X.
- **Spanx:** Hide & Sleek Cami—S–XL.
- **Yummie Tummie:** Freedom T Tank has minimizing panels to smooth waistline from bust to hips; extra long length avoids ride up.
- **Yummie Tummie:** Crew and V-neck T-shirts; bra lines, torso, and upper arm slimming under any lightweight knit.

tip The dearth of flattering/nonfattening arm lengths and sleeve shapes in T-shirts is aggravating at best. Most manufacturers really don't understand the flattering sleeve issue. Unless an arm is slim and toned, caps or lengths that draw a line across the bicep are fattening. I buy my favorite T-shirts in long sleeves and take them to my drycleaner to shorten to anywhere from just above to just at the elbow. Plays up a slim forearm; disguises the rest.

And while we're on the subject: In general wear sleeves to shave off a good five pounds visually. Unless your arms appear smooth and toned (front and back), I don't recommend sleeveless tops, straight-cut round or square-cap sleeves or girly and tight puffed sleeves that draw a horizontal line smack through the fullness of the upper arm. The cruel irony of sleeve treatments that are meant to look young is that they expose skin that does not. Best to cover full upper arms, cellulite, sun damage, and skin that has lost elasticity. Instead, create the illusion of sleeker and longer arms with skimming three-quarter lengths and blouses or dresses with a kimono, or bell sleeve (to name but a few). Always have a look at which new sleeve shapes offer the right coverage.

- ▶ **Show some shoulder:** A portrait neckline that slides off a shoulder or a short evening jacket or shrug that reveals a bit of the shoulders in a strapless dress while covering the arms is always youthful. As designer Donna Karan once said: "No woman ever gained weight in her shoulders."
- ▶ **Layering to look leaner and longer:** Lighten up; keep your layers lightweight or you'll look padded. Combining very fine-weight knits does the trick, but there is a limit to the number of layers one should wear at one time. Layering two thin T-shirts, a camisole, and the odd cardigan or jacket looks more rumpled than off-the-cuff chic.

Avoid weird proportions

- ▶ **Long over short:** Your top or tank should never end right at your waist/waistband or you'll visually saw your body in half, exaggerating full hips and bottom. Nor should the outer layer of a jacket or cardigan hang significantly longer than the under layer. What looks most flattering (and modern) is a difference of no more than two inches between the outer and an untucked under layer. This one can be tricky since manufacturers sell all kinds of awkward combinations.
- ▶ **Too long:** Beware any layer that falls too long on the leg. In an attempt to mask a full bum and thighs, many women opt for midthigh-length tops. Visually, a long top shortens the appearance of your legs, which makes you appear larger and square.
- ▶ **Short over long:** Critical. Choose an under layer in the same color or tonality as your outer layer or you'll create a fattening horizontal line at your hips or bottom. Keep the shapes skimming. A cropped jacket cut to widen to an A-line hem in a firm fabric should be layered over a narrower piece that has a little drape, skim, and softness. If the jacket hem is straight, your top can flare slightly (if it flatters you), but in general if your top is similarly narrow, it will keep the look long and lean. Most of us would rather pass on additional volume at our hips.

Transparency

It is critical to anchor any transparent top with a completely matte and supportive foundation piece underneath. Shiny bra top camisoles or bodysuits will make you appear larger. A dress or top with sheer illusion sleeves can make full arms appear smaller, but pay careful attention to the sleeve construction. It should have a close-fitting (not tight or loose) armhole and should meet the edge of your shoulders. Be sure the sewing is not visible and that sleeve fit is skimming, not straight, full, or baggy. Baggy is fattening.

And ...make a smooth transition

The point at which your top and bottom meet should be smooth from every angle. Getting the proportions right with a top that is either tucked in or skimming over a waistband is the difference between looking longer or blocky. You will always look slimmer when your top meets your bottom at the high hip.

> tip Smooth-topped and pocketless pants with a side zipper are hard to find. If you find a flattering cut with a good rise and a side zip, grab them in a few colors. These are ideal under tunic-length tops.

your stylist's lower body checklist

For Pants

WAISTLINE: I favor a waistline that rests just below the navel to the high hip for missy sizing and at or just below the navel for plus sizes. These are flattering for a rounded belly, rises drawing a line through the fullness and rather than molding it with fabric creating the illusion of a flatter stomach. Some manufacturers still cut pants with 10-inch rises and waists that hit up to an inch above the navel. Their thinking is that when a waistband hits where a woman is narrowest it will make her feel shapely. How else to explain "Mom jeans"? A waistband that sits above your navel combined with a long rise accentuates rather than camouflages a rounded belly.

HIGH-WAIST PANTS: These are not reserved for the tallest and slimmest women. Look for a flat front and a wide waistband (a panel that rests at or just above your navel at the top and up to an inch below at the bottom). When waistband fabric is doubled it creates a little corset effect, and this, combined with a skimming fit though the hip and a full-cut leg looks longer and leaner. Don't confuse these with styles that have an exaggerated high waist or cinch-belted waist ('40s Kate Hepburn style by way of '70s) that reach an inch and some above the navel. These are best left to the flattest of tummies—of any age.

A UNIVERSALLY FLATTERING CUT: Grazes the hips and over the bottom—just snug enough for a defined shape—and then falls into a straight, medium-to-wide leg. Wider cut legs elongate the leg. How wide is right for you will depend on your height, but petites should also look for this cut, sized proportionately. If your pant has a crease down the center front of the leg, you'll look longer. To balance any hip or thigh sensitivities, this is your cut.

LOOSE IS BETTER: Remember, whenever you are on the fence about a trouser size in a woven fabric—particularly with little or no stretch in the fabric—always move up a size. Have a tailor nip in the waist or hips slightly so that the fit is truly skimming and has a nice, smooth drape over your curves. The slightest pulling anywhere is— you guessed it—fattening.

PROPORTION AND BALANCE: The eternal rule of thumb—the slimmer your pants, the fuller your top can be. Which is why the boho-chic combo of a midthigh-length tunic or a short dress over pants is a slimming favorite of full middles. The wider your pants, the more tailored or close to the body your top should be.

POCKETS: Make sure pockets are in a flattering location. A vertical pocket along a side seam makes most women's hips appear wider. Pockets that are angled diagonally or vertically on the front of the pant are flattering for most.

THE RISE: Ladies, honestly I cannot tell you how many women I see wearing the wrong length rise. Too short and grabby and you'll deal with tummy bulge, sharp creases across your lap, and worse still . . . camel toe. Too long and the look is droopy—which usually means the pants are too big all over. Your legs look shorter; your bottom looks bigger; and who wants bagging across their abdomen? The overall visual is, of course, fattening. When you next edit your closet, group any offenders into a charity pile. Recutting a rise is tricky business, an expensive tailoring job, and is seldom successful.

sure, wear shades of white

Yes, even ladies with ample bottoms can wear white pants, with a few provisos:

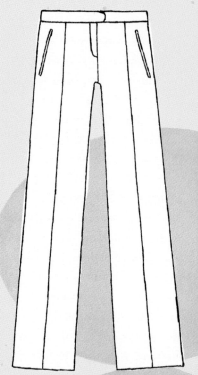

- **Fit:** Buy white (and other light neutral shades) a little looser than usual. You want skim between the fabric and your undergarments. Too tight and white is both revealing and fattening. Remember that the brighter the white, the more of a focal point you create with your lower body.

- **Fabric:** Should be as matte and opaque as possible. White denim is an appealing and less revealing choice.

- **The cut:** Should fit you as described above. Not even the slightest tapered ankles, or you'll create a light-colored barrel on your lower body.

- **The pockets:** Hip pockets are widening—especially in white. Better to sew them closed. Baste those back pockets and remove any pocket linings that hang over your derriere like two flags of surrender.

- **Underneath:** Keep in mind that many inexpensive pants and contemporary lightweight pants are unlined. Lining fabrics like lightweight cotton, linen, or silk interfere with smooth drape. Wearing white underpants under a white bottom is a "No," big time. They show through clear as day. Thongs also are a bad bet. If you have even a quarter cup of cottage cheese on your bottom and thighs, it will show through. Not to mention that thongs offer zero support. Wear a panty that closely matches your skin tone. Lycra and spandex styles that skim over your belly and have an under-the-cheek-hugging fit will flatter your rear view better than cotton pants. When more intervention is needed, try a midthigh to midcalf shaper with a control top.

JEANS: Really tight jeans are fattening. Baggy jeans are very fattening. A jeans fit requires a balance unlike any other pant. Good fit is also affected by the relative stiffness of denim as compared to woven fabrics with soft drape. Too stiff and you'll develop deep creases in some very unflattering places. Too "washed" or relaxed and the fit can look droopy and dumpy. Jeans should glide on and then hold you in— just a bit—across your bottom and stomach. Denim with a little bit of mechanical stretch (meaning Lycra or spandex is woven into the cotton) can change the landscape. They should fit snug at the waist (or have a little nip at the tailor to make that happen) and over the hips, ease over your bottom, and fall fluidly into the cut of the leg. No cupping or creasing under your cheeks. Good fit, dark denim, and a shoe-grazing length will make you look longer and leaner. A sure thing.

HEM: Hem your pants to wear with at least a 1-inch heel to lengthen your line and raise your rear view. The pants and jeans that you rely on for anything from a casual workplace to a low-key evening out should brush the top of your shoe. Pants and jeans that are strictly casual and that you wear with flats can measure anywhere from just above the anklebone (straight leg openings only) to the top of your foot. Calling all capri-pant-loving ladies: Be sure to get the length right on your leg. Just like a skirt of the same length: Midcalf, horizontal lines foreshorten your legs and give you a thicker-looking line. Try on lengths that are a bit shorter or longer to best judge where your legs look their longest and leanest. If pants don't have a side slit, have a tailor add this visually lengthening detail.

THE SHORTS REVIEW: Slip into your favorite pair and then sit down in a chair placed in front of a full-length mirror. Watch what happens across the crotch, at your stomach, and your thighs. If they are cut at midthigh length, chances are you won't like the wider and shorter look of your legs. Shorts with pleats are particularly unflattering.

A BETTER LOOK: "City shorts" that have a skimming fit through the hips with a length at just above or just below the knee. Same principle as your ideal knee-length in a skirt. The rear view will be flattered by a cut that is snug and smooth across your low back and that skims over your bum. Any pair with a fit that cups under your bottom is a pair you leave in the fitting room or throw on a charity pile during a closet sweep.

Skirts

I recommend knee length. Your particular length may fall just below the knee, through the knee, or just above the knee. The point at which your legs appear their longest and leanest is right—regardless of what is featured in magazines and on selling floors at the moment. The knee length for you will also depend on your knee sensitivities. If you've drawn a "Great Legs" ticket in the genetic lottery, by all means create a focal point there and raise your hem a bit. The visual appeal of the average knee is somewhat fleeting. Your ideal length—skirt by skirt—depends on proportion, your legs, of course, the construction of the skirt, and the heel height that looks best with the cut of the skirt. Best to work out the length with a good tailor.

It's a fashion myth that legs are the last things to go. If you are not crazy about exposing yours, don't bother with skirts at all. Wearing lengths at midcalf will accentuate full calves and make you appear shorter and heavier. Models are the only women on the planet who don't appear shorter and perhaps frumpier than they'd like in midcalf lengths. Concentrate on the most streamlining effect you can create with well-cut pairs of pants. Witness Hillary Clinton; she has developed a uniform with her pants (suits) that covers legs she clearly prefers not to expose.

Any skirt you choose—from knee length to beach-resort ankle length to a floor-grazing evening skirt—should have a close-to-the-body fit over your hips without any clinging or creasing. The waistband—presuming there is one—should have a little ease. The tighter a waistband (or the tighter any belt), the wider your hips will look. Not to mention the flesh roll that sits above a band or belt pulled too tight. Whether the style flares or remains straight at the hem, as long as the upper portion is skimming, you will look trim and nicely elongated.

PENCIL SKIRTS: Should always have a close-fitting waist and an ever-so-slightly pegged bottom. The intent is to enhance or finesse an hourglass shape. Wide hips and a full booty look shapelier when a garment skims the curves. Straight is the enemy of voluptuous girls. A straight skirt creates a visual line that travels—at the same width—from your low hip (for most, their widest point) to hem. Very fattening indeed.

A-LINE SKIRTS: Styles constructed from panels instantly minimize and disguise lower body volume—but be certain that there is a skimming fit and drape from your waist and over your hips or your skirt will widen your appearance.

PLEATS: Inverted pleats stitched flat from waist to high hip and that originate from a smooth-yoked waist will disguise full hips and thighs. A soft inverted pleat placed at the center front will disguise a full abdomen.

tip   Traditional waistbands—sewn with a separate band of fabric—have gone the way of the girdles that used to be worn underneath. The sewn-under waistbands of today tend to gap at the low back and spin around the middle. As there are more attractive and productive uses of your day than righting your waistband, best to bring any offenders to a good tailor. The addition of darts is the best way to create a snug fit at your waist and hips. That low-riding skirt look is passé except in the halls of your local middle school.

DRAPING: Diagonal draping across the abdomen and over hips offers masterful concealment of a full abdomen. Draping that meets a panel of pleats at hip level is twice as nice.

SIDE SLITS: Look saucy paired with great gams. Just the kind of subtle focal point you may want to employ. However, front slits are the antithesis of grace in motion. They bunch, they crease, fabric moves between your legs. Altogether a bad bet visually, if not potentially embarrassing.

AND FINALLY: A skirt should always be longer than it is wide. That kicky Lacroix-esque pouf resembling a French maid's skirt should be donated to the costume department of your community theater.

Strategic Placement

Look for these "classics of camouflage" when you shop:

ASYMMETRY: Whether a neckline, hemline, or a panel sewn into the shape of the garment, diagonal is lengthening and slimming.

BIAS: Fabric that is cut on the diagonal. While bias-cut silk slip dresses can be exceptionally molding and revealing, bias-cut tops and dresses in matte stretch wool, for example, offer a fit that shapes and lengthens.

COLOR BLOCKING: There are color blocks we can create for ourselves when, for example, we wear a black jacket with a white top and pants. The light underpinnings create a long vertical line. Then there are clever color blocks that designers install in their clothes as focal points for added shaping. For example:

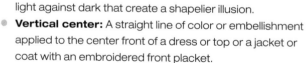

- **Bright or multicolor shapes** at a neckline, an inset in a bodice, or placed on the diagonal across a bodice or at the hip.
- **Dark shapes or wide bands** placed on a light color at the waist or along the torso for waist whittling.
- **Geometric or floral prints with dark pattern** placed at the waist, hips, and across the derriere. These are the prints you want!
- **Vertical or curvy diagonal panels:** Dark against light or light against dark that create a shapelier illusion.
- **Vertical center:** A straight line of color or embellishment applied to the center front of a dress or top or a jacket or coat with an embroidered front placket.

DIAGONAL DRAPE: The ne plus ultra of flattering illusions:

- **Small busted?** Choose DD in a top, dress bodice, or bathing suit.
- **Full tummy?** DD over your stomach and abdomen camouflages the fullness.
- **Short waist?** Wear a top or dress with DD that begins at the neckline and extends to the hips for a torso-lengthening illusion.

FABRIC: Flattering fit is entirely dependent on the character of fabric:

- **Stiff:** Fabrics are only flattering for skirts that require a little presence.
- **Texture:** Heavy and thick textures make the body in them appear heavy and thick.

- **Shiny:** A reflective surface looks bigger than a matte surface. Shiny silk tops and scarves create flattering focal points. Shiny stretch satin dresses, skirts, or pants create shiny and wide-looking focal points. Choose matte muted metallic if you want to wear a little shine on your bottom half.
- **Clingy:** Tissue-weight cotton and lightweight cotton with lots of stretch show every line and bump. Yes, even in dark colors.

SPACING: Pay attention to how any pattern or print is spaced. Closely spaced, two-color graphic patterns will read like a textured solid. Midsized prints—particularly in a vertically drawn design—are slimming. A print of exploded shapes or flowers spaced far apart will make you appear larger.

SHIRRING: Look for sleeves, swimsuits, or skirt tops with a little shirring—rows of stitched gathers that run parallel to a seam—to create an effective and soft drape that hides bits and bumps.

RUCHING: At a neckline, hemline, and trim, such as: ruched ribbon placed vertically on a jacket front or edge trim, or fabric ruched into a double ruffle on a shirt front.

let's talk about color

Coco Chanel once said, "The best color in the whole world is the one that's right on you." By now, we know what colors we like. We all have a natural affinity for certain colors and not for others. And we've all had time to work out the obvious stinkers—any color that suggests hepatitis C or air-sickness pallor has been swept from your closet long ago. And still, here is what I see every day: women dressed in colors (and neutrals) that suck the very life's blood from their skin.

There are different (and often complicated) takes on how to wear color to look slimmer, to boost skin tone, and to create focal points. Mine is neither lengthy nor is it complicated but I find that my abbreviated view is very effective for choosing clothes for shoots for clients and for myself. Learn to use color to your advantage. Experimenting with new colors—and, yes, trendy colors when they suit you—especially next to your face, is central to dressing your body better. Wearing the right colors has been a secret weapon of ageless women since the ancients.

First, there are three universal characteristics used to describe any color:

▶ **Hue:** Defines a color's undertone—which is either warm (yellow-based) or cool (blue-based). Your skin's undertone will be either warm or cool, and so will the colors that flatter you.

▶ **Value:** Refers to the depth of a color and a grading of that color from darkest to lightest. You may look splendid in a vivid value of a color and not so splendid in a muted, softer value of the very same color.

▶ **Chroma:** Defines the clarity of a color. Some colors are vibrant and light-reflective; others are muted or dark and absorb light. Fabric also determines if light is reflected or absorbed. Wool will always seem to suck up light, creating a matte (and slimming) surface, while satin or silk with sheen will reflect it (visually widening).

Here's how I have used these distinctions to guide me at work and in my own closet. In my early career, I watched how great makeup artists created individual, blended, strong, or subtle color palettes for the models. I asked them lots of questions about why they used some colors and not others. From them I learned that you must take a very close look at skin in good daylight to determine its undertone(s). They will be predominantly yellow or blue. Yes, we all register some pink, or blue-red, or orange-red too. But the clearest guideline is the predominance of warm or cool. Eye color also has subtle undertones like gold, brown, green, or blue—warm or cool flecks—that further influence which shades will look most flattering.

On photo shoots, I am as focused on the model's skin, eye, and hair color as I am on her height and proportions. When a model arrives at the studio in the morning—sans makeup—with a quick glance I can see what colors will flatter her coloring. But until I hold individual shades up to her skin and eye color, I don't choose her outfits for the day. Just as makeup artists mix and blend colors specifically to complement the model's natural undertones, whether cool or warm, I've learned that a shade that makes her skin look vibrant in daylight—without a lick of makeup—will create the most beautiful image under studio lights. It is no different for any of us in real life. The more precisely we identify the shades that flatter us now, the better we look.

Try this in daylight and with no makeup (this is a marvelous motivator for a full-scale closet edit): Make piles by color of things you wear most and things you don't wear much at all. One group at a time, hold each piece to your face and watch the effect. Think about the hue, the value, and the chroma as you separate colors that make your skin look vibrant from the ones that make it look flat, your eyes look bright or dull; which make under-eye shadows look more or less noticeable. Make a pile of what you think looks most flattering.

tip Even if you know your Color Me Beautiful "season" from the '80s or you've been color-printed over the years at cosmetic counters, it is the here and now of your coloring that counts. Just as our hair color goes through a hormonal progression from childhood to adolescence to the first grays of adulthood and perimenopause, so does our skin. The undertone of your skin may be similarly affected by hormonal shifts and climate. Many women find that their undertones change with age. Factor in your skin's loss of elasticity and the surface dullness that occurs with less estrogen. Just as you use effective products to improve the quality of your skin, you can amplify that youthful effect with the colors you wear. Use them as a reliable gauge for your current hair color and makeup color. Does everything look harmonious right now? What might benefit from a little change?

stop neutrals abuse

How to Wear Black

Poor black. No other neutral is as misunderstood and misused. Fashion extols the timelessness of black, the versatility of black, the chic of black, the mystery of black, and, of course, black's power as a light absorber that hides our ticks and bumps. All true. Also true, it is time to take a careful look at the effect of black flush to your face and neck. Black looks splendid when it is combined with black. White, gray, and rich colors like warm and very deep browns, reds, and blues also make winning companions for black. Especially since the minimalist '90s, black has become every wardrobe's fallback position, often resulting in some truly unappealing combinations: pale, soft knitted bootie pink, baby boy blue, and newborn chick yellow should never mix it up with black. And those sun-bleached colors like pale mauve, sage green, or washed terra-cotta are bilious with black. Worse still, bright colors like purple, turquoise, or fuchsia look dulled down next to black, whereas next to gray, brown tones, or whites they look vibrant. Ladies, black is not a crutch. It's a very specific look. Entirely its own thing. Cultivate a few skin-flattering combinations underneath that black jacket or paired with black bottoms and watch your look become more sophisticated instantly.

How to Wear White

White ranks as the next most abused neutral. White is not merely white. It may have undertones of soft gray or blue, light yellow, palest pink, or cream. If your skin is cool, then white as bright as snow or cool as a glacier will positively sing against your complexion. If it is not, you will look like you need a hug and a good nap.

Warm-toned ladies should favor off-whites: cream, ecru. Bright white makes you look ashen. Never trust white to store lights. Undertones are barely discernable, so keep those price tags on until you hold up your new white in daylight. You'll know you have a winner if your skin and eyes look bright.

Slimming Color Combinations

MONOCHROMATIC DRESSING: Fashion 101. Wear one color to look longer and leaner. It is a guaranteed result. Problem is, most of us do this with black, and it can look very draining. Instead, try monochromatic combinations of dark colors that flatter your skin tone. Or be sure that you use black as a bottom or an outer layer.

A white blouse and a black skirt is a time-tested standard of chic, but it will also divide you in half visually. To maintain a long, unbroken line, try wearing your shirt under a dark jacket or cardigan. You maintain the slimming dark outline and add a surface texture to the look. Your stylist's preferred riff on monochromatic dressing is a rich and dark color mix. For example: Prussian blue, French blue, or midtoned navy on top, black on the bottom. Deep wine, grape, raisin combined with soft grays are other subtle variations that draw color next to the face and neck and create a lengthening vertical line on the body.

In a truly global fashion market, it's always summer somewhere. This is good news for women who dress for warm weather year round, as softer colors are now part of the scene in fall/winter collections. To keep pastels such as ice blue, blush pink, lilac, peach, or mint green looking chic and ageless, combine them with white, off-white, khaki, taupe, and camel. Monochromatic or tonal pastel combinations are generally too much pastel. They have to be handled very skillfully or acquired from a designer who has combined them very skillfully. And that usually means there will be a print of pastels thrown into the mix and paired with the sophistication of a neutral (other than black).

Tonal Combinations

Choose one of your most skin-flattering colors to create combinations from lightest at the top to a midtone meeting point (created by your outer layer or a wide belt) to darkest at the bottom, to ground your look. For example: a pale gray top, strands of midtoned gray pearls and beads that draw the eye to your face, worn with a dove gray cardigan, jacket, or belt that creates a smooth transition between top and bottom, combined with a bottom of charcoal. Add a third color—in a slightly softer or darker value—as an accent. Necklaces and scarves are always an individualistic way to bring colors together and draw the eye upward.

tip   For monochromatic and tonal combinations with pants, extend the lengthening line with a shoe that matches your hem. Wear a black shoe or a strong color and the eye is drawn straight to your feet. In skirts, wear either nude legs and nude shoes/sandals or opaque tights in a close tonal combination with your skirt hem and shoes for a lengthening leg line. In general, black and very dark shoes are a bad bet for mature legs, ankles, feet, and the attendant spider veins that look positively livid next to them.

3 dressing for your shape

Now that we've talked about the power of good fit in a general sense, it's time to concentrate specifically on the best shapes and proportions for your shape.

Here is a simple excercise. For my returning clients from *The Pocket Stylist*, this will serve as an update, and it is an essential starting point for new clients. You'll need a full-length mirror, a tape measure, and a chair. The next time you are wearing a favorite outfit—for example, your favorite pants, your best-fitting jacket or button-front shirt—take time to rotate slowly in front of a full-length mirror. Slip on a pair of heels to elongate your body line and slowly turn from front to side to back and back around to front, paying attention to how your clothes look from every angle. Our clothing is in constant motion with us as we move through the day. Walk in place, stretch, reach, bend. Take note of the fit of your clothing, how the fabric moves on your body, paying close attention to:

- Where buttons close
- Across your bust
- Bra lines—front, sides, and back
- Around the armholes, sleeves, and across your shoulders
- Across your stomach
- Across your crotch

Now sit in the chair facing the mirror and look at:

- Fabric across your torso/stomach
- Across your lap—belly and upper thighs

And finally, as you stand up again, watch how your clothes either fall back into a shape or stand away from the body and look stiff and deeply creased. Any place that is visibly tight, grabbing, gapping, loose, or bagging will visually break up your body into a series of unflattering bumps and creases. No woman's preferred look. Developing your eye for the shapes and fit that will compliment your body depends on visualizing yourself as you move through your day, wearing certain shapes and not others.

Next, slip out of your clothes (a bra and panties is fine), but please keep on those heels and stand in front of the mirror again. Imagine lengthening your body; gently square your shoulders and take more than a moment to turn around slowly. Front, to side, to back, to face front again. Notice the 360-degree circularity of your body as you move. No scrutinizing whichever body part(s) you think is throwing things off, please. The elemental truth about your body in clothes is that you are dressing your bone structure first. The frame you are born with is your natural silhouette. Embrace the idea of dressing for your silhouette instead of just covering up parts.

Now let's focus on the shape of your torso. Notice the width of your shoulders in relation to the width of your hips. It is this "torso silhouette" that will basically determine the clothing shapes that are right for your body. Naturally, the size of your neck, breasts, waist, and belly will all factor into a more refined profile of your body type. But that comes later. Honor your natural structure, learn to wear only the shapes and proportions that balance your upper and lower body first, and learn to either accentuate, suggest, or merely skim over what happens through your bustline and waist.

In my nearly twenty years of styling photo shoots and creating wardrobes for individual clients—both famous women and "civilians" (as we noncelebrities are called) alike—I've encountered the same three torso silhouettes that illustrate three basic body types—A, B, and C, as I call them. Body types D, E, and F have the same basic proportions as A, B, and C but represent plus-sized bodies.

- Is the width of your shoulders and torso smaller than the width of your hips? **You are a type A.**
- Are your shoulders and your hips roughly the same width, with a defined waist? **You are a type B.**
- Is the width of your shoulders the same or slightly wider than the width of your hips? **You are a type C.**

Keep in mind that body types D, E, and F represent women who are fuller variations of A, B, and C. Body type D is a voluptuous, full-fashion

version of body type A, E of B, and F of C. You can be a body type B and wear a size 6 to 8 or a body type E and wear a size 14W to 16W and your best shapes and focal points will essentially be the same. At any size, your torso silhouette—your frame—offers an accurate initial determination of the shapes that will create a longer-looking balanced body line.

Take another good look at your entire body and notice the spatial relationship between all of your parts. Now I will ask you to take your measurements and write them in the appropriate spaces below. For the most accurate read, take your measurements after lunch (when we all experience a little fluid retention).

- **Shoulder to shoulder:** From the edge of one shoulder to the edge of the other shoulder.
- **Bust:** Under your arms and around the fullest part of your chest.
- **Natural waist:** At your navel.
- **Low waist:** Approximately one inch down from your natural waist.
- **High hip:** Four to five inches from your natural waist.
- **Low hip:** Eight to nine inches from your natural waist.
- **Thigh:** At its widest point.
- **Rise:** Measure from natural waist down to crotch, holding the tape a little loose, through the legs up to waistband back; repeat for low waist.

Why bother with this? Because from now on, I suggest that you shop with a tape measure and your current measurements at hand. For bottoms in particular—but with any piece of clothing that you are unsure of—measure things first.

Try this the next time you shop for pants or a slim skirt. Run your tape measure across the low hip and multiply by two. Then measure the rise at the natural or low waist, dependent on the construction. If the measurements match or are close enough to yours, then move on to the fitting room. If they do not, try a size smaller or larger. Don't worry about the size on the hangtag. Sizing for the mass market is an imprecise science at best. The only way to assess good fit is by looking at shapes first and sizes second. You will also want to feel the fabric. Give it a little tug to determine if the fabric has a little stretch to hug your body or little give.

Another compelling reason to have your measurements at hand? Online retailers and catalogues provide very accurate size charts for their merchandise. Matching your measurements to their sizing is the only way to order good fit—particularly if you are a woman who shops special sizes (petite, petite plus, tall). If you take the time to measure things first, you may never again find yourself in a fitting room with a size that appeared right on the hanger and had your size on the tag, only to find that the fit is truly wrong for you.

Your edited list of bottoms, tops, jackets, coats, and dresses will include the right shapes and proportions to complement your bone structure and to create an optimum Almighty Unbroken Body Line. Our sizes will naturally go up and down, and with them lengths will go up and down, widths will widen or narrow, seasonal colors, textures, and details will infuse things with "now," but the shapes and proportions you'll look for in any season (and in any year) and the silhouette balance they provide will remain essentially the same for life. Simplifies things, right?

for all body types

If You Are Long-waisted

Our additional balance remedies for you will focus on choosing bottoms that visually lengthen your legs while raising the appearance of your waist.

▶ We'll avoid crops, capris, anything with a tapered bottom, and especially very low waists (time to edit any offending jeans), and any cuffed hems. All of these styles will make your torso appear disproportionately long in relation to your legs.

▶ We'll choose high-waisted pants that visually raise your waist a few inches and thus lengthen your legs by a few inches. Tucking in your shirt will continue the leg lengthening line. Pants hemmed to graze the top of your shoe and worn with even a small heel will elongate and improve your line.

▶ We'll choose cropped jackets in interesting colors to pair with tonal or monochromatic combinations of tops a few inches longer than the jacket hem and that cover the waistband of fluid pants.

▶ We are also shopping for slim, straight skirts at just-above-the-knee length. If it flatters you, we'll add a midwidth to wide belt at the waist to raise your waistline. Skirts are one of your best bets, as the eye can't read where your leg begins as it can in a pair of pants or jeans.

▶ We're looking for empire waist dresses to visually lengthen your lower body, along with either straight or   skirts with plenty of drape.

If You Are Short-waisted

Since our height is perceived by the length of our legs, you have a lower body that looks leggy and is probably relatively easy to fit. Our balance remedy for you will be choosing tops that elongate the line of your torso for a more proportionate look overall.

▶ We'll choose tops that fall below the waistline of your bottoms to your high hip. If you want to tuck in a shirt or soft blouse, it has to be of a lightweight enough fabric to blouson slightly over your waistband or belt.

▶ We'll lower or remove the belt loops from your pants so you can wear a belt below the waistband. Wide belts in particular should be worn an inch or two below your natural waist to lengthen your torso. Matching the color of your top and belt is another torso lengthener to try.

▶ We'll also lower the belt loops on any jackets or coats that wrap to make your torso appear longer.

▶ We'll add deep V-necks, shirts worn unbuttoned to your waist and worn over a tank, long-length necklaces, and long oblong scarves to your shopping list.

▶ Sheath and shift styles worn at the knee work for you. If you add a belt, it must be the same color as your dress (or a very close tonal match) and drop it down a few inches below your natural waist.

specific tips for petites

For All Body Types 5'4" and Under

▶ While it is possible to find pieces in regular sizes that will work for you, it's best to start with petite or petite-plus sizing. A design team has worked out the proportions for you so that finding the right fit hopefully is not a struggle. Altering missy or full-fashioned sizes that have been proportioned for an average height range to petite proportions is costly and generally unsuccessful. Shortening things alone won't do the trick, as details like button placement, pockets, and pant rises will all fall too low on your body.

▶ Narrow silhouettes and fabrics that drape will offer a skimming fit that flatters. Full shapes and stiff fabrics will give you a boxy line and make you appear shorter.

▶ Choose monochromatic and tonal color combinations to achieve an unbroken vertical line. Spark a monochromatic look with a combination of fabrics and textures, top and bottom. Sharply contrasting colors top and bottom will make you look shorter.

▶ Prints and patterns should have a vertical design that draws the eye up and down rather than across your body. Look for smaller-scaled, two- or three-color graphics and prints sized no larger than the palm of your hand. Oversized patterns and exploded multi-color floral—even when you can find them to fit—will overwhelm your silhouette.

▶ Horizontal details such as breast and hip pockets on jackets and coats, double-breasted coats, stripes, pant cuffs, ruffled or embellished hems, and jackets that fall at your low hip will all shorten and widen your silhouette. Look for vertical details—single-breasted jackets and coats, slit pockets set on an angle, zip-front jackets and coats, color blocking that employs vertical lines, narrow to mid-sized vertical stripes.

Now let's turn to your body types and begin.

you have

- Small to medium frame
- Narrow or sloping shoulders
- Small to medium bust
- Narrow torso and ribcage
- Small, low waistline
- Full lower hips and bottom
- Full legs

Your midlife fit challenge: You gain and hold weight in your lower body. If your belly is full your lower body looks disproportionately round and wide in relation to your upper body.

our plan

We're looking for tops and jackets with visual interest to draw the eye upward. Shoulder details, horizontal necklines and strong lapels combined with shaping horizontal and vertical seams will subtly widen the appearance of your upper body in relation to your lower body.

We'll choose bottoms in crisp fabrics that create a minimizing straight line or an A-line, as well as fabrics that drape over your curves. Your tops should always meet your high hip or just above to avoid any pulling where your upper body and lower body meet.

what your wardrobe should never be without

Pants

Trousers: Flat front with a straight, stovepipe leg and a skimming fit from a waistline at or just below your navel. Try a wide waistband (about 8") to smooth over a full tummy. Key to a streamlined look: a skimming (snug but not tight) fit over your hips and upper bottom and a smooth full pant leg. Features like besom pockets placed just below the waistband on your trouser front and welt or "faux" welt pockets on the upper back of your pants are subtle and sleek looking. Opt for styles sans cuffs unless you are a tall type A.

body type A

Wide legs: Work for average height and tall type A's providing they fit like your trousers. Be sure to choose fabrics that drape over your curves.
Jeans: Your best bets will be either a bootcut or a "boyfriend" cut, or stovepipe leg like your trouser. Again, choose close and shaping fit over your hips and a full leg opening to avoid a wide appearance. A contoured waist is ideal, no tapering ankles and no cargo pockets.

Skirts

A-line: In fabrics that drape worn at knee length. Always choose a snug and skimming fit from your waist to your hipbone to avoid a widening effect. Casual A-lines are an ideal substitute for shorts or crop pants that may exaggerate the proportion of your lower body. Try an inverted center pleat to draw the eye up and down with a lengthening vertical line.
Circle: A small waistband or no waistband and darts for shape to create a smooth fit over your belly and very soft drape over your hips. Opt for soft fabrics only and wear at knee length with heels.
Sarong: Or a skirt constructed to look like one with a soft diagonal drape across your tummy and hips, worn at knee length for day. Ankle lengths are best for medium height to tall type A's.

Tops

Look for horizontally placed details at your shoulder or neckline like pin tucks, yokes, piping, buttons, flowers, appliqués, and embellishments. Small-scale prints and patterns, and horizontal and chevron stripes flatter.

- **Tailored shirts:** With a skimming fit and seams, darts or panels to create shape. Avoid anything boxy or oversized.
- **Wrap tops:** In cotton broadcloth or knits for soft drape worn at hipbone length. Key to your best appearance: The shoulders must fit well; have a tailor remove any excess fabric under your arms.
- **Bateau, ballet, or square necks:** A skimming fit and a hem at high hip will visually broaden your shoulders and lengthen the appearance of your torso.

Jackets and Coats

Your jackets and coats should fit your shoulders precisely, meaning that the seam extends just past your natural shoulder. The addition of a dolman shoulder pad will broaden their appearance. Essential to the look: a skimming fit through your torso and sleeves. Pass on any jacket or coat that swamps your upper body to fit (or cover) your lower body.

Nipped waist jacket: With vertical seams to suggest your waist. High collar, a yoked shoulder, peaked or wide lapels, important buttons, color, and texture draw the eye upward. Opt for single-, two-, or three-button styles meeting your high hip or slightly above. Skip hip pocket details unless they are set at your high waist.

Blouson jacket: Soft blousing at a band resting just above high hip. Works well with all your bottoms.

A-line coat: Set-in shoulders flaring slightly from under arms to hem. Empire or a high waist with soft gathers or pleats where the torso meets an A-line sweep. Double- or single-breasted and knee-length creates an ideal silhouette.

Trench: Strong yoked, epaulettes, double-breasted and belted just above your natural waist. Look for styles with a full skirt and an inverted back pleat or a deep back vent for a flattering A-line silhouette.

Dresses

Empire: A waistline just under the with a full and A-line skirt in fabrics with lots of drape.

Shirtwaist: A tailored shirt bodice and full A-line or circle skirt. Best worn at knee length. Keep it modern. No retro or girly prints.

Wrap dress: A bodice that fits like your wrap top with a full and draped A-line. The look is most successful in fabrics like matte silk viscose and in subtle prints.

---

tip Wear the highest heels you can manage comfortably to lengthen your leg line. A regional or seasonal consideration: Avoid visually slicing your leg into thirds when you wear tall boots. Wear opaque tights in the same color as your boot to cover the slice of knee exposed between the hem of your skirt and the top of your boot for a longer and leaner look.

type

A looks

you have

- Small to medium frame
- Average to broad shoulders and back
- Average to full bust
- Small to average defined waist
- Average to curvy hips the same width as your shoulders.
- Teardrop shaped, average to full bottom
- Shapely legs

Your midlife fit challenge: When you gain weight, you tend to gain top and bottom. So, while heavier, you remain fairly proportionate. Even if your torso and has thickened a bit, never lose sight of your waist in any outfit. Belt it or suggest it with pieces constructed of seams, darts, and panels that create a nipped waist and an hourglass shape and structure.

our plan

We're shopping for shapes and proportions that will emphasize the well-proportioned balance between your shoulders and hips and that compliment your curves. Key to the success of your look: The curvier you are then the simpler the shapes and details must be to avoid making you look heavier than you'd like. We are looking for bottoms in firm fabrics with a little stretch that will create a minimizing straight line or an A-line along with tops and bottoms constructed in soft fabrics that will drape over your curves.

what your wardrobe should never be without

Pants

Trousers: Flat-front styles with a cut that skims your shape from waist to low hips with a straight, stovepipe leg. Try a wide waistband set-in at low waist to minimize a full tummy. Whether you are shopping for full lengths, ankle length, or crops like "city" shorts at knee length, this is your bottom-flattering shape. The fuller your bottom then the greater the need for simple styling and a full leg opening. Skip vertical hip pockets or stitch them closed. Raise the focal point to your waist with a thin belt.

body type B

Wide legs: Wide leg styles can work for petite, average, and tall B's alike providing that the fit is snug (not tight) and skims smoothly over tummy, hips, and the top of your bum. A smooth and line-free transition into the leg ensures the look is flattering.

> tip Avoid skinny cuts like cigarette and toreador pants altogether as they will make your hips and bottom look wide. Watch out for any too-slim cuts that cup under your bottom. Not your preferred look.

Jeans: Bootcut or stovepipe or "boyfriend" cuts in dark denim with a little stretch offer hip and bottom balance. Try rises from navel to low waist. A contoured waist that rises a little higher in the back prevents "muffin top." Close and shaping fit over your tummy and hips and bottom are critical.

Skirts

Pencil: A just-below-the-knee length and a slightly tapered hemline compliment a curvy shape. Fabrics like midweight stretch or seasonless 100 wools are ideal. If your torso is fairly trim, try a style with an attached wide waistband for hourglass definition.

A-line: With a waistline that rests at the navel or just below and just-below-the-knee length. Good for you in both firm wool and crisp cottons for a defined shape. Fabrics that drape will create a curvier effect.

Circle: A small waistband or no waistband and darts for shape. Key to the fit: a smooth fit over your belly and hips. Choose soft fabrics only.

Tops

The fuller your bustline then the simpler the tops you should wear. Keep details and prints subtle to avoid looking blowzy.

Tailored shirts: Styles with vertical seams, darts, or panels that look shapely, not blocky.

A soft blouse: Minimal details and a skimming fit in fabrics with drape like matte silk, silk chiffon, and cotton voile. Low U- and V-necks compliment your curves. Simple and full sleeves disguise full arms.

T-shirt styles: For day or night, shapely styles with a knitted-in nipped waist in fabrics like cotton jersey, cashmere, and wool blends.

Watch out for silk knits as they expose every line and bump, and look baggy and fattening. Hipbone lengths and three-quarter sleeves have an elongating, slimming effect.

tip Be sure your tops have enough length to tuck into skirts and blouse slightly over your waistband to disguise a full midriff and maintain a focal point at your waist.

Jackets and Coats

Nipped waist: Choose vertical seams for installed shape and a panel sewn in at waist level for shaping. Attached belts and sash belts are good for you too. Single-breasted styles with a very low stance are best for smaller-breasted type B's. The higher stance of a two-button style is better for fuller busts. Your jackets look best hitting at either hipbone length or just clearing your bottom.

Bomber jacket: In supple leather, suede, soft wool, or sweater knits. Look for constructions with a sewn-in panel at the waist to suggest a belt. Avoid anything oversized or boxy.

A-line coat: Look for styles with set-in shoulders and a vertically paneled construction to assure a feminine shape. A belted waist and at-the-knee length always looks right. Straight coats are deadly on type B's.

Trench: a variation of the construction above. Look for styles with either an inverted back pleat or a deep back vent for a full, sweeping skirt that will accentuate your belted waist.

Dresses

A variety of dresses work for type B's but the common denominator is that any style should have waist definition.

A-line dress: Varying styles from a bloused top to T-shirt simple and a full A-line body. The silhouette is achieved in fabrics with drape and with a belt.

Shirtwaist: A simple shirt bodice attached to a full A-line or circle skirt.

Belted sheath: A good option, with the effect of a top tucked into a belted pencil skirt.

Bias-cut: A good option. Fabric cut on the diagonal suggests the waist and makes a full skirt hang more gracefully.

type

B looks

you have

- Average to broad shoulders equal to or wider than your hips
- Medium to full bust line
- Straight, short to average waist
- Straight hips
- Often a flat, rather than rounded bottom
- Slim legs

Your midlife fit challenge: When you gain weight it is generally in your midriff and belly and you may lose your waist altogether. If you have a short waist, it is especially hard to find a skimming fit that doesn't make you appear thick and straight.

our plan

We're after shapes and proportions that will help you finesse a more hourglass shape. This starts with tops that skim and deemphasize your shoulders and middle combined with pants and skirts that create the illusion of a curvier bottom. We want skirts and dresses that create shape and drape at your hips and create a focal point at your slim legs. Constructions that place your waist at just above or just below your natural waist will create the illusion of a longer torso.

what your wardrobe should never be without

Pants

Your straight hips and slim legs provide you with a number of pant options in varied widths and lengths.

Trousers: Whether skimming and slim or midwidth and stovepipe, they work for you. Low-waist or no-waistband styles with darts visually lengthen your torso. Hems that graze the foot and ankle lengths are good for you. A slim trouser shape works for at-the-knee "city" shorts as well.

Jeans: Try a contoured waistband rising slightly higher in the back than in the front for waist and hip shaping. Narrow and straight, stovepipe width and bootcuts are all good options for you in denim with a little stretch for added shape.

body type C

Skirts

There are many styles that work for you. Combined with very simple and solid tops, you can wear color, pattern, and embellishment to create a focal point at your lower body. Here are your stylist's favorites for you:

Torso skirt: An A-line shape with inverted pleats or soft gathers attached to a smooth, close-fitting yoke that rests at the low waist. Adds a bit of shape and drape to your hips and bottom and creates a focal point at your legs.

Stitch down pleats: Look smooth across the belly and flirty across your hips. Just about any pleat will work for you with the exception of any updates on the dirndl—a style with full gathers at the waistband and an awkward bell shape.

Trouser: With a flat tab front, zip fly, and slashed hip pockets worn at low waist. Snappy looking with a button front and safari pockets.

> **tip** Patterned bottoms work for type C's of all heights. Look for midscale prints, plaids, and embellishments placed on the diagonal for a curvier effect.

Tops

Keep things simple and avoid details at your shoulders such as tight armholes, peaked or puffy gathers, buttons, epaulettes, and appliqués. Strong horizontal necklines like square and bateau will also exaggerate their width. Here are your best options:

Tailored shirts: Constructions with vertical seams and side panels for a more defined middle. You can also pull off fuller, seam-free cuts that clear your bottom, worn over slim bottoms. Look for contoured hems for a more finished and bottom-flattering effect.

> **tip** Ruching along a center front seam minimizes a full bust and midriff.

Pullovers: V-necks and U-necks at midchest or above. Best in supple and lightweight knits like cashmere, merino, cotton jersey. V-neck cardigans hitting from hipbone to below your bottom will make your torso appear longer. Pair with tees or tanks that are proportionate in length. Avoid short under long combinations that will make you look heavy.

Surplices: Good option for a soft blouse style with a deep V and diagonal drape across the bust and midriff; suggest a slimmer and longer torso. Good in silks, silk viscose, rayon jersey.

Jackets and Coats

Nipped waist jacket: Natural shoulders with a high cut arm for the look of a longer torso. Single-breasted styles with small to midwidth lapels hemmed at high hip to just below your bottom.

> tip Choose a low stance to create an elongating V-line from your neck to midchest (for fuller busts) or between the breasts (for smaller busts).

Cardigan jacket or coat: A collarless and uncomplicated straight cut and worn open. Hip level pockets are good for you.

Peacoat: Semifitted and double-breasted with a structured mid-width notch collar. Go for a monochromatic match of coat and buttons and a high hip length. Brassy buttons will give you a blocky look.

Classic coat: Single-breasted for a lengthening vertical line and a subtle A-line shape. Go easy on buttons and skip any shoulder or breast level details. Create visual interest with good fabric and color.

Dresses

Straight and A-line shifts: A skimming fit at knee length. If you wear dresses, never be without some current variation of this silhouette. For evening, a lower cut neckline will create focal points at your bust and your legs.

Surplice: A soft variation on the wrap dress that works for short waists. Same fit principle as your surplice top and attached at the low waist to a straight or A-line skirt.

Shirtdress: In fabrics such as cotton broadcloth and silk and worn unbelted or belted at the low waist.

type

Clooks

you have

- Narrow or sloping shoulders
- Medium to full bust (proportionate with your shoulders)
- Full, high defined waist
- Wide hips and a full, round bottom
- Very full thighs and calves

Your midlife fit challenge: You hold most of your weight in your lower body. If you have a full belly your lower body looks disproportionately large and rounded in relation to your upper body. Key to creating a longer and smoother-looking silhouette: a clean transition where your top and bottom meet without any pulling, bunching, or riding up.

our plan

We're after tops and jackets with visual interest to draw the eye upward. Shoulder details, horizontal necklines, strong lapels, and constructions with both horizontal and vertical seams for shaping will subtly broaden the appearance of your shoulders as a visual balance for your lower body. Also on our list, pants cut in a minimizing straight, full line and skirts with subtle A-line drape.

what your wardrobe should never be without

Pants

Your best choices will be flat front with a minimal waistband for a smooth appearance under your tops. If you struggle with gapping waists, have a tailor add darts at the back of your waistband to give you a better, curvier fit.

Trouser: With a straight and full leg for a visually slimming and lengthening look. You want a skimming fit over your bottom with enough ease and drape so that there is no cupping under your cheeks. Fabrics like firm, good-quality double knit ponte and lightweight wool and rayon with a little stretch are good choices.

body type D

Yoga/pajama pants: Any pull-on style with a flowing full leg, a smooth and gather-free waist or a drawstring set into a flat waistband. Tonal combinations of top and bottom create the illusion of a longer torso and lower body length and a proportions balance. A good option in linen, rayon silk for weekend and resort dressing.

Jeans: Look for styles with a contoured waist rising higher in the back and slightly lower in the front for better fit, wear at your navel or just below. Straight and full stovepipes or bootcuts should ease over your hips and create a minimizing straight line from waist to hem. Best in dark, stretch denim. No tapered ankles and no cargo pockets.

Skirts

Your skirts should fit closely at your waist and over your tummy and hips and move into a subtle A-line shape. A just below the knee length is best. Skip any skirt that is ankle length and straight for day or night.

Gored skirts: Wide, vertical panels sewn together for an A-line shape that drapes and skims over your curves. Flattering for type D's of all heights worn at knee length. Best paired with tops or jackets hemmed at high hip for a smooth line.

Flared: An A-line with center front and back seams in draped matte jersey.

Stitch down pleats: Thin, vertical pleats in lightweight rayon silk create a smoothing drape and the illusion of a narrower bottom. When they are in style, A-line broomstick skirts in dark gauzy fabrics are a great hot weather or resort option.

Tops

Choose set-in sleeves to visually widen your shoulders with arm-holes that are full enough to avoid any pulling across your bust. Add a dolman shoulder pad to your tailored shirts to better define your silhouette. Create a focal point with details at your shoulder or neckline such as pin tucks, yokes, piping, buttons, flowers, appliqués, or embellishments.

Tailored shirts: With a skimming fit in stretch cotton broadcloth. With rounded shirttail or side slit hems to avoid pulling or riding up over your waistband.

Wrap tops: For day, try stretch cotton broadcloth, matte silk, or silk rayon. The diagonal front drape adds shape through your torso and volume to your shoulder line. Choose color, vertical stripes, contrast collars and cuffs, French cuffs for details that draw the eye to your upper body. Look for styles that extend the line to high hip with a "skirt" attached to the body of the shirt. Shirts hemmed at a just-below-the-navel length won't flatter you.

Bateau, ballet, or square necks: With a skimming fit to visually broaden your shoulders worn at high hip for a smooth look.

Jackets and Coats

Finding styles that fit your lower body and won't swamp your upper body can be a challenge. Here are the best options:

Cropped jackets: That fit your shoulders and skim the torso. Details like wide lapels, rolled collars, and collarless necklines place a broadening line at the shoulders. Look for contoured hems that hang longer in the front and the waist in the back.

Fit and flare coat: With armholes placed just outside your natural shoulder line. The combination of an empire waist attached to an A-line skirt made of vertical panels installs flattering shape for your lower body.

Swing: An ideal style for sweater coats. Modern-looking in flat or vertically textured midweight knits and with elongating details like vertical border trims. Wear at high hip or fingertip lengths.

Dresses

Empire: Fitted over the bust with a flattering deep V or U neckline. Sleeves like kimono or bell extend your shoulder line. You want a style with a full skirt, gathered at the center front and center back or constructed with a deep inverted center pleat. Good in heavy to midweight matte jersey, rayon chiffon, and matte stretch silk.

Shirtwaist and wrap: With a bodice styled like your wrap shirt or a skimming and tailored button front shirt attached to a full A-line skirt. Good fit on top with a full sweep at the skirt make these ideal for you.

type

you have

- Average to broad shoulders
- Full, round neck
- Broad, often rounded back
- Full, rounded bust
- Full, defined waist
- Broad hips
- Shapely legs

Your midlife fit challenge: When you gain weight you gain top and bottom so, while heavier, you remain fairly proportionate. There are a few visual tricks for you to consider. First, choose necklines and jacket closures that create a deep V-line to draw an elongating vertical line from your neck to your waist. Second, never lose sight of your waist. Try soft sashes and thin belts placed at your low waist. If you prefer to skip a belt, suggest your waist with pieces that have seams, darts, and panels for shaping.

our plan

We're looking for shapes and fabrics that drape over your curves and accentuate your natural hourglass shape. We'll keep your tops and bottoms clean lined, minimally detailed, and constructed in curve-loving fabrics with stretch and drape.

what your wardrobe should never be without

Pants

Trousers: Are best for you with a flat front and a full straight leg. You want the waistline to rest at your navel or just below. Fit your hips and bottom first. Size up when needed to clinch a skimming fit. Have any excess at the waist removed at the tailor.

Jeans: Look for styles with a contoured waistband rising higher in the back than the front for a fit that works with your curvy hips. You want a snug (not tight) fit at your waist and high hips and a full stove-pipe or bootcut leg. Choose unadorned denim. Skip embellishments and cargo pockets.

body type E

Yoga/pajama pants: With a smooth, gather-free waistband or a drawstring set into a flat waistband. You want straight and full legs in very lightweight wool or good-quality linen with drape to skim over your tummy, hips, and bottom. Tonal combinations of your top and bottom are visually lengthening and slimming.

Skirts

Pencil: Straight and tapering slightly at the knee for shape in double knits like ponte, stretch wool, and midweight stretch cotton twill.

A-line: With a waistline that rests at your navel or just below and a just-below-the-knee length. Good for you in fabrics that drape to avoid a wide or blocky effect. Try styles with an inverted center pleat to draw the eye up and down.

Gored: Medium to wide vertical panels create an A-line drape over your curves. Choose fabrics that move with your body like matte jersey, rayon, and cotton.

tip   If your skirts tend to hang lower in the front than in the back, it means your waistline is sloped. On the set I've rolled and pinned the waistband in the front (yes, some models have sloping waists too) to fix the problem. This works in a pinch covered with your top or a sash belt and layered under a jacket, but this is best solved at the tailor.

Tops

The less detail on your tops the better. We want a long, unbroken line for your upper body. Skip breast pockets and go easy on ruffle fronts unless they are thin and placed vertically on a front placket, or diagonally on a top with drape.

Tailored shirts: Choose fabrics like stretch cotton broadcloth, silk, and good-quality rayon. Look for lightweight cottons like voile for a softer look. Key for the fit: darts at the bust and full armholes to avoid any pulling across your shoulders or bustline. Look for styles with vertical seams placed front and back for a shapely fit.

Pullovers: With V-necks, U-necks, and ballet necks. Choose mid-weight cotton jersey, cashmere, and wool blends for a cling-free and skimming fit. Watch out for silk knits (especially in light colors), as they expose every line and bump and can look baggy and fattening.

> tip
> Hipbone lengths and three-quarter sleeves create a slimmer and longer effect.

Surplice or wrap tops: A good option for a soft blouse style. The deep V-neck and diagonal drape across the bust and midriff create the illusion of a slimmer torso. Good in silk, stretch cotton broadcloth, silk viscose, and rayon jersey.

Jackets and Coats

Collarless: With a nipped waist or soft sash belt. Look for a clean placket front for the illusion of a longer and slimmer upper body.

Blazer: With a nipped waist, a skimming fit through the torso and sleeves. Good with all your pants and skirts.

Peacoat: A semi-fitted and double-breasted style with a structured midwidth notch collar. Choose a monochromatic match of buttons and coat fabric to keep the look streamlined. Brassy buttons will give you a blocky look.

Wrap coat: A curve-flattering cut in supple fabrics that drape from sweater knits to lightweight wool and alpaca. Best with soft, set-in shoulders and either collarless or with a small shawl collar. For greater ease through your shoulders and bustline, try a version with either raglan or kimono sleeves.

Dresses

A-line: A soft blouse or T-shirt simple bodice attached to a full A-line skirt. Best in fabrics with lots of drape like matte jersey, silk viscose, or rayon chiffon for evening.

Shirtwaist/wrap: A simple tailored shirt or wrap shirt bodice attached to a full A-line or circle skirt. Again, in fabrics with lots of drape.

type

E looks

you have

- Full neck
- Broad or rounded shoulders
- Full to very full bust
- Broad rib cage and a full torso
- Undefined, full waist (often short)
- Full, straight hips and a flat bottom
- Slim legs

Your midlife fit challenge: You gain and hold weight in your midriff and belly. A combination of a full (or very full) bust and a short waist makes it hard to find a skimming fit that does not make you appear full and straight. Dressed in the wrong shapes, your upper body appears disproportionately wide in relation to your narrower hips and slim legs.

our plan

We're looking for constructions that are straight or slightly A-line. Tops with an easy and skimming fit are on our list. We want to smooth over your bust and midriff without pulling or bagging. We're after flattering necklines and interesting details that draw the eye upward. Bottoms with narrow legs are also on our list. However, we'll avoid very tight legs that will make your upper body appear larger in relation to your lower body. We'll look for necklines and hemlines wih interesting details placed on the diagonal for a slimming effect.

what your wardrobe should never be without

Pants

Slim trousers: A narrow leg is your best option. Look for styles with a stitched-in or pressed-in center crease to accentuate your slim legs. Cuts with a side zipper and a little elastic placed discreetly at the center back of the waistband create a smooth finish under your tops.

Crisp cotton twill, silk shantung, and firm double knits like ponte work well. A fuller leg of the same essential shape works for taller type F's. Hem length is critical. Narrow, straight legs look best hemmed to brush the top of the foot or shoe.

body type F

Cigarettes: This is a flattering cut in seasonless stretch wool and firm silk for a sleek-looking line. Always have current pair of these in black—for day and evening—in your closet and you'll always have something to wear. This cut looks terrific hemmed at ankle length.

Jeans: Look for styles with a contoured waistband rising slightly higher in the back than the front for a snug (not tight) fit at your low waist and through your bottom. Slim and straight or bootcut styles are both good for you. Dark and white denim work for you.

Skirts

Straight: Look for a cut with small gathers at a thin waistband for a shapely, smooth fit over your tummy and hips. Look for details like side slits to create a focal point at your gams.

Trouser: Cut in firm fabrics with a little stretch. Any fly-front zipper should lay flat against your tummy. A great style to pair with a long cardigan that falls just under your bottom.

Stitch-down pleats: Thin pleats stitched into a minimal waistband give this straight shape a slimming vertical texture. Nice for daytime in crisp cotton and for evening in lightweight silk.

Tops

Tunics: Fabrics, necklines, sleeve shapes, and embellishments change the look of this flattering shape. Try a just-below-your-bottom length with pants and a just-below-your-belly length for slim skirts.

Tailored shirts: Key to your best fit: deep armholes for ease across your shoulders and bust. Go for unadorned, unfussy styles.

Pullovers: U- and V-necks, asymmetric necklines cut on the diagonal, and deep side slits at the hemline all create a longer and leaner look. You want a very skimming fit with plenty of drape over your middle. Best in matte jersey, midweight cotton jersey, merino, and cashmere.

avoid Big shirts or oversized camp shirts with shoulder seams that fall on your upper arm. You'll look swamped and oversized. Any neckline that gaps is a neckline you'll leave at the store or send to the tailor.

Jackets and Coats

Cardigan jacket: A collarless and easy silhouette worn open over a skimming top. Simple textures and vertical trims or embellishments along the jacket opening will visually elongate your torso. In sweater knits choose solid colors and subtle patterns and smooth or thin, vertical stitches.

tip The two hem lengths should be proportionate for a flattering line.

Shirt styling: An ageless and classic layering piece. Look for contoured shirttail hems or hems on the straight with deep side slits. Best in a just-below-our-bottom length.

Car Coat: A straight or slightly A-line shape and a natural shoulder. A single-breasted style or a covered placket keeps the look smooth and lengthening. Current-looking collar and sleeve treatments and interesting fabrics give this classic a hit of "new."

Dresses

Shift: In fabrics with soft drape and worn at knee length. Look for modern variations of this classic with interesting hem and neckline treatments.

Shirtdress: A tailored shirt style unbuttoned to midchest for an elongating V-neck. Choose a style with side slits for ease and a focal point at your legs.

type

F looks

4 ageless
trendsetting

"Live long enough and you will have seen
it all and worn most of it."

—Diony Farr (my mom)

By the time we reach our 40s we've seen (and worn) many of the trends that resurface time and again. If we've learned anything, we are interested in current ideas that will last for a few seasons rather than five-minute fads. At their best, current trends are the result of designers reexamining the familiar themes and classic pieces we've all worn, but reinterpreted with a new spin. The remixing of silhouettes, retooling of proportions, experimentation with new fabric technology and treatments, new combinations of color, print, and texture allow new currents to break through fashion's surface. This is, of course, why "new" is so much fun—and who wants to stop having fun with her clothes at any age?

Wearing something au courant makes us feel plugged in to now and, sometimes, vividly connected to our younger selves. Should we revisit a trend we've worn before? Sure, but only in a modern and subtle incarnation. Flashbacks are never a success. We all should skip any literal recreations of the looks we loved then. We're interested in style evolution, after all. At this point in our conversation you might very well ask your stylist, "Since trends come and go so quickly, how much do I really need to pay attention? I want to find a few good-looking and current pieces each season—I want to look fabulous, not like a fashion casualty." And you would be right.

Women with ageless personal style remain true to themselves first. They will always choose the most current interpretations of their shapes, lengths, and best colors. They have developed a few uniforms of their preferred mix of feminine shapes and masculine tailoring, their favorite combinations of investment pieces mixed with less expensive things. They have an interest in what's new but wear trends selectively, never slavishly. Paying attention to what is current will streamline your wardrobe by moving it along a few new pieces at a time.

With more to look at—more brands, subbrands, celebrity-designed lines, and indies piling on every season, it takes the focus of a Galápagos hawk to pluck out not only what fits but looks modern and relevant. *Relevant* is the operative word here: Looking relevant transmits that you are plugged in. In a culture obsessed with quick impressions and with youth, you can use your own personal style to communicate to the world that you pay attention to all kinds of cultural currents and that you are curious and embrace change—and this includes your appearance as well as your outlook.

Some of you may be thinking, "I want to look young, and I don't see what's wrong with wearing some of the same things my daughter wears. I want to look cool and fun." Cool? If we are talking about millennial-style cool, in my opinion most of the looks are too derivative to be taken seriously. We've all worn this stuff before in some iteration. You've got your own cool, and your daughter might learn something from you. Also, if you're old enough to have experienced the fashion of the '70s, you don't need to be told about cool.

But let's talk a bit about fun. I'm all for it—but not for wearing things that have clearly been designed for someone in her 20s or younger. These are easy enough to spot—the themes are numbingly consistent from year to year: Hippie, Rock, Grunge, Prairie, School Girl, Sexy Secretary, Pole Dancer, Geek. You can express a youthful attitude without wardrobing yourself in any of the these defining looks. But let's face it, ladies, it is not easy to find the kind of fit and luxe sophistication one finds in high fashion just anywhere. It takes paying attention and digging.

We over-40s spend more time than any other female consumers cherry-picking racks of the irrelevant, the inappropriate, and the banal to find what of the new will work for our wardrobes and our bodies now. You have a far better chance of finding the best design—in any price range—if you have a clearly defined image of what you are going for. Homing in on only those new pieces that will flatter your shape is always your starting point. Period. As for a little research, fashion magazines are an obvious source for taking in the looks of a new season. Remember, however, when what's featured doesn't relate to your life, it's their disconnect, not yours.

High-fashion designers will always include a few unwearable, museum-worthy showstoppers in their runway shows to inspire the attention of the fashion editors who will include them in the stories that will create edge and excitement and that will sell ad pages. The business at hand is fantasy and aspiration. Reality is not their concern here.

So thumb through the pages knowing that you are making mental notes—a piece here and there—for a sense of the clothes that will relate to your body, your lifestyle. Don't get bogged down with the subplots detailing which trends are worn by which actresses, singers, supermodels, retired supermodels, or socialites. Our cultural fixation on what celebrities wear is irrelevant to our process. And, please, I implore you to disregard any "style" advice found in tabloid magazines. While they may provide a diversion during a pedicure, they are not fashion oracles. Getting "The Look" is what it is all about in their orbit. The Ageless Woman couldn't care less about "The Look." She's only interested in "Her Look."

Here's how the Ageless Woman takes on any season:

▷ She understands that the silhouettes in any trends cycle will change far more slowly than the colors, prints, or embellishments that designers use to make things look a little different every few months. There are only so many variations on shapes and themes in fashion's pantheon anyway. When you have found your best combinations, stay with them; update them.

▷ She pays attention to the overarching themes, whatever they may be: floral prints, menswear, knit dressing, metallic fabrics, and so forth, focusing only on what looks sophisticated. Then she scrutinizes how she will adapt "new" to suit her needs.

▷ She knows that trends are reinterpreted from decades past and it is fabrics that provide the true novelty in a season. Notice how color and surface texture can transform an updated but time-tested shape into a piece that looks unexpected and modern. A few examples: a trench coat in neoprene (scuba fabric) is both futuristic and classic at the same time; a shirt jacket made in metallic jacquard elevates a workday staple to a piece with go-anywhere potential; sporty staples like a windbreaker or an anorak take on a sly elegance when cut from silk or taffeta. These "double agents" have a high and low versatility that is essential in a wardrobe.

▶ She looks for sophisticated color combinations. She knows that a graphic print or an abstract floral, for example, looks newer (and more grown-up) in unexpected colors.

▶ She looks closely at the subtle but defining details: stitching, pleating, draping, buttons, or piping that add a quick-change element to her proven shapes—just enough—so that they'll nudge things along in her wardrobe.

▶ She wants her clothes to create a distinctive complement to the statement accessories: an up-to-date shoe; the classic handbag she's resurrected from years ago; bold costume pieces, old and new. All these articulate her personality and individuality.

Fashion moves at lightning speed. There is no longer one right way to look—for day or night—and frankly we're all grateful we're not required to practice the prescriptive dressing our mothers and grandmothers knew. There is, however, a right way to choose from what's available if your goal is to create ageless chic in your closet. Since the distinctions between ageless and aging can be subtle, your stylist has chosen ten trends for their seemingly endless appeal to designers and us. These ten classics of the trends landscape are consistently reworked (and worked over) at all price levels from luxury to "mass-tige":

Trend:
the little tweed jacket (Chanel-ish)

Long before the rest of la mode caught up to her modern sensibilities, Coco Chanel created one of fashion's most essential (and ageless) pairings: chic clothing in utilitarian fabrics (like wool jersey and tweed). Chanel's clothes offered a sharp (and comfortable) contrast to the constricted silhouettes of the day and her look stood out as always youthful and modern. She was the original architect of ageless style.

Chanel borrowed more from her lovers' closets than their knit cardigans and tweed hunting jackets. Inspired by the ease and mobility of men's clothes, she crafted her early suits in knit jersey surplus (made for men's underwear). The suits that defined her comeback in the '50s were cut in tweeds. Tweed bouclé (or buckled surface) has a miraculous quality for flattering a woman's shape. Practical and camouflaging, tweed is firm enough to define the shoulders, shape the torso, and smooth over the midriff, and soft enough to provide complete ease of movement. Although richly textured, the look is bulk-free.

The Chanel cardigan jacket is a one of the dominant strands in fashion's DNA. Mademoiselle once said, "Fashion is always of the time in which you live." Karl Lagerfeld has headed the house since 1983, and in twenty-five years he has reinterpreted the jacket innumerable times, enhancing its relevance by combining the little jacket's traditional lines with his keen eye for the "street." The Chanel jacket has evolved without compromising its inherent elegance. Every season, designers—from avant-garde to the affordable—will borrow from (or subvert) the jacket's simple but distinctive lines. Of course it's a status thing—or the suggestion of status—but never mind the pedigree. Regardless of the provenance of your jacket or its cost—if it's worn well tailored, the look will always convey a timeless image of chic.

Trend:
floral prints

In the early twentieth century, haute couture and contemporary art began design collaborations that resulted in the first truly modern prints. Although most were originally created for evening dresses, their scale and inventive use of color inspired the repeat prints we consider modern looking a century later.

In the 1950s floral prints reflected post-war optimism, as they transformed from naturalistic blooms to an explosion of flamboyant floral abstraction. Christian Dior—although best known for his love of solids—created a memorable floral of red and green roses named the Caracas dress. Equal parts South American vivacity, French haute couture, and landscape painting, the dress is preserved in the collection at the Metropolitan Museum of Art. The woman who wore a Dior floral was no shrinking violet, nor should you be. For the timeless and ageless approach: Look for abstract or art-inspired blooms, unexpected colors, and uncomplicated shapes.

Trend:
animal prints

Lion, tiger, zebra, giraffe, cheetah; animal prints are a part of fashion's wildlife year round. Season after season, they evoke instant glamour combined with graphic pop. But of all the animal prints in fashion's repertoire, the ageless and timeless queen of the fashion jungle is the leopard print.

Sophisticated, nervy, sexy: Think vintage Sophia Loren, every inch the Italian movie star in a leopard dress; or Hitchcock's heroine Grace Kelly facing the glare of flashbulbs in dark glasses and a sporty leopard fur coat; and, of course, Anne Bancroft as Mrs. Robinson in *The Graduate*, the seductive proto-cougar in leopard lingerie and sheer stockings.

Leopard is the print with legs—managing to be chic, racy, and practical. The uniformity of its graphic pattern flatters all shapes and sizes. It's right, day or night, providing that you allow the print to do all the talking (or growling, depending on the setting). Wear shapes that are clean lined—whether current or vintage. Dolce & Gabbana's signature leopard print was inspired by 1940s and '50s screen sirens like Loren. Their signature print is a constant in their collections, confirming the philosophy that no woman should be without a little leopard in her wardrobe. Wear-anywhere pieces like the soft button-front shirt, the sheath, the satin tunic, the trench coat, the topper—all anchor the Dolce & Gabbana look. At Christian Dior, John Galliano has been known to take license with his leopard by recoloring it in shades of emerald and gold and black and gray.

Crib (or buy, if you can) from the animal prints at the top as a standard by which to judge the best-looking leopards at lower prices. Be assured that designers all the way down the fashion food chain are doing the very same thing.

Trend: knits

Fair Isle, fisherman, chunky cable knits, delicate pointelle, or jersey; most of us could illustrate the story of our lives just with the knitwear we've worn over the decades. But the ageless and timeless approach to wearing knits draws from what looks right now rather than anything nostalgic, sweet, or faux vintage.

In the 1930s, Coco Chanel (yes, a great many of fashion's modern silhouettes were innovated by Mademoiselle) introduced the twinset—a matching cardigan and sweater—and its slouchy silhouette looks as relevant today as it did then. Designer Madeleine Vionnet began cutting knit jersey on the bias in the same period, creating a new drape and curve over the body. In the '40s, American designer Claire McCardell invented the casual jersey knit "leotard," dressing that Donna Karan would reinterpret in the mid-'80s, offering working women a chic system for dressing as essential as menswear.

Fit, texture, pattern, and color: Knits add it all to our wardrobe. The twenty-first-century mantra of effortless personal style is made easy with knitwear pieces that offer comfortable stand-ins for tailoring.

Cashmere, merino, and jersey are all ideal in seasonless weights. What is changing the range of our current choice (besides global warming) is new technology that produces textural-looking yarns that feel ultralight on the body. New, refined knitting techniques mean less weight and more defined shapes. Good-bye to anything baggy, boxy, or bulky. Knits are ideal for integrating color and texture into your wardrobe, an easy way to mix patterns to suit your individual style.

Trend: menswear

Marlene Dietrich once said of herself, "Darling, the legs aren't so beautiful . . . I just know what to do with them." This may explain why in 1932, the Paris police took umbrage at one of Dietrich's strolls along the Seine dressed in a man's suit. She also famously donned custom-made tuxedos. Clearly she understood one of the essentials of timeless personal style: the power of tailoring—that a precise line is the best way to project a stronger and longer-looking silhouette. Every female body benefits from the definition and structure of a great suit. A well-tailored jacket creates shoulders and lengthens and narrows the appearance of the torso and arms. And there is nothing like a pair of precision-cut pants to create the illusion of a longer leg and a smaller bottom. Smolder and swagger: female curves in blade-sharp tailoring like Hepburn's and Garbo's in their World War II trousers. Naturally, the look remains forever provocative to fashion designers, who never tire of the androgynous allure of menswear. However, the look veers into cliché with too many masculine accents in one outfit. Think more Armani than vintage Annie Hall; more Ralph Lauren than the louche retro glamour of Madonna in her send-up of Dietrich in pinstripes and a satin bustier. Skip the bow ties and bowlers, neckties and fedoras. While charming costume drama for younger women, the timeless approach relies on something more direct and far more potent.

Memorable interpretations (among thousands): Bianca Jagger in her signature white Yves St. Laurent Le Smoking; Helmut Newton's 1975 photograph of an androgynous beauty standing on a dark and deserted Paris street clad only in a black YSL tuxedo (what else did she need?); Lauren Hutton in pants and a vest in the Charlie fragrance ads; Ralph Lauren's decades of feminized menswear looks; Calvin Klein's minimalist suits. And memorable for the wrong reason: Céline Dion's 2000 Christian Dior Oscar dress: a white floor-length "backward tuxedo" dress with ropes of pearls, a fedora, and sunglasses.

Trend: military

Peacoat, sailor pants, trench coat, safari, flight and bomber jackets, and windbreakers: They represent a distinct fashion lexicon and a series of images relevant to fashion since World War I. There is debate among fashion historians about who introduced the "pea jacket" as prêt-à-porter. Some sources credit Christian Dior and his interpretation of the jackets worn by the French navy. Most attribute the look to Yves St. Laurent, whose chic gloss on the sailors' peacoats he found in New York City Army Navy stores became a wardrobe staple of fashionable women around the world, including Catherine Deneuve, Lauren Bacall, and socialite (and international clotheshorse) Nan Kempner. St. Laurent's military-inspired designs (including the trench and safari jacket as well) defined the blend of masculine and feminine that continues to inspire designers today.

While women in the '60s created a style for bomb throwing—literally and figuratively—clothed in the counterculture cool of real Army Navy surplus, and the women of the late '70s found their uniforms in the military-issue combat boots and torn fishnets of the punk anarchist, it's the classic adaptations of enlisted men's military uniforms embellished with officers' buttons and trims that capture an ageless and timeless chic that is pure personal style.

Trend: metallics

If metallic fabrics make you think of Elizabethan costume dramas or 1930s screen sirens in "liquid lamé" gowns or maybe the wardrobe of Liberace in his Vegas heyday—well, you'd be right on all counts.

Lamé—French for "leaves of silver and gold"—is an ancient weaving technique that creates a shimmering background or patterns such as brocade or jacquard. Lamé brocades looked groovy in the '60s and lamé spandex loved the nightlife and discos of the '80s, but not until the early '90s were metallic textiles widely embraced by fashion as a day-to-night wardrobe solution.

The new century's look is defined by structure. Functional pieces and simple shapes take on a different quality entirely in fabrics with luster. Coats and jackets cut in metallic fabrics or gilded leathers are the *completers* that every woman needs in her arsenal. A perfectly tailored metallic is wardrobe gold and pulls together any outfit of solid neutrals: navy, ivory, chocolate, denim, and, of course, black. For daytime, choose fabric with a low-watt sheen, a burnished look, or a textured surface to wear as you would any neutral.

Here is a golden (or platinum, pewter, or bronze) rule for day or night: the brighter the shine, the more detailed the surface texture; the more ornate a design, then the more starkly simple the silhouette must be. Tight, short, heavily embellished, voluminous, or oversized and boxy will tarnish this look. An exaggerated silhouette or too many details is gilding the lily.

Trend: global inspirations

Western culture's love affair with exotic goods from the far reaches of the globe is centuries old. More recently, fashion's love affair with the grab bag of global inspirations known as boho-chic can be traced to the late '60s and to the legend of Yves St. Laurent and his peasant-inspired looks in ornamental, rich fabrics. At the same time, New York designers Oscar de la Renta, Giorgio Sant'Angelo, and Stephen Burrows each defined the look in the United States.

Here's a brief review of the origins of many references we see again and again on the selling floor:

FUNKY: Putting things together that are exciting and unique that wouldn't ordinarily be seen as working together. The passion for vintage clothing was born from the desire to mix beautiful and real fabrics with authentic things from other cultures rather than wear mass-manufactured, synthetic fabrics.

ROMANTIC: Defines a look that first hit big circa 1968 with fashions inspired by the Orient; by odalisques and the harems of the *Arabian Nights*; by India and its draped saris; by early nineteenth-century Empire dresses—often all blended together (funky romantic). The Romantic look became so all-encompassing it can be represented by three subcategories:

- **Hippies:** Levi's; Indian leather fringe; headbands; love beads; Indian gauze dresses; hair long and straight, often impossibly matted with straw.
- **Rich hippies:** World-traveling compatriots of hippies too stoned to change their jeans. Style nomads who embraced a mix of gypsy shifts, peasant smocks, and zouave pants; African and American Indian tribal patterns; Moroccan caftans; Afghan sheepskin coats; South American ponchos; pieces inspired by Russian ballet; necks, arms, shoulders, and waists loaded with exotic jewelry and accessories from all over the world. Hair impossibly wavy and gorgeous, often adorned with silk scarves and peacock feathers.
- **Ruffles and ringlets:** Brocade jackets; velvet knickers; ruffled-front shirts and cuffs; ruffled dresses in sheer prints with milkmaid sleeves; hair worn in ringlets or tied in ribbon bunches.

For our purposes now, anything with the patchouli-scented whiff of hippie or ruffles and ringlets should be bypassed. Gauzy, excessively ruffled and tiered, dragging-on-the-ground sun-dressy, fringed, all this drag is as uplifting as wilted lettuce on mature bodies. Remember, the softer our bodies become, the more structure our clothes should provide (subtly). Clothes should not droop. Droop, she is not ageless.

Look modern (and fight gravity) with straightforward simplicity. Choose shapes, patterns, and embellishments that lift the eye upward and that don't fight for the spotlight. The ageless and cultured nomad will always combine a little Western tailoring (by way of New York, Paris, or Milan) with her flights of Eastern-inspired exotica.

Trend: lace

From paintings of Renaissance Madonnas resplendent in golden guipure to a twentieth-century Madonna crawling across a video set in black poly-stretch, the look and texture of lace has been intricately woven into the pattern of feminine dress and decoration for ages.

Lace was one of fashion's first big status items. Fifteenth-century lace-making centers like Venice, Antwerp, and Brussels flourished, and hundreds of lace patterns defined the style of their countries and counties of origin. In the sixteenth century lace was à la mode worn as elaborate collars, cuffs, and ruffs. Fashion favored the flounced hem in the seventeenth and eighteenth centuries and by the nineteenth century, the birth of machine-made lace assured that ladies of lesser means could wear it for the first time.

Brides, first cocktail dresses, prom dresses, birthday party dresses—lace is largely nostalgic, as most of us can remember at least one beloved piece. Now, however, it's best not to look backward. Skip any lightweight poly-laces that simply hang on the body. Walk on by any lacy party dress that reminds you of your Gunny Sacks or Jessica McClintock frocks from the 1980s. (Shockingly enough, I frequently see flounced, lace "prom dresses" for grown-up ladies in dress departments.) Lace plus frou-frou is a no-no.

Lace plus streamlined shape equals ageless. Lace looks daytime modern made of firm cotton or wool (which offers the added benefit of smoothing over lines and bumps). Examples: Black lace backed by beige functions as a graphic pattern; brown, beige, navy, gray, or brown-hued pastels all read as textured neutrals that will add surface interest and verve to monochromatic or tonal combinations. Be sure that the lace has a little heft in your hand. The fabric should have enough oomph to retain its shape.

Let's chat briefly about lace's cousin eyelet. She looks fairly straightforward and adult in dark-colored cotton and sufficiently sophisticated and fresh in a simple white button-front shirt. From time to time she surfaces in laser-cut black wool or linen for an interesting dress or skirt effect. However, eyelet is a toothache in girly pastels, and she is positively shrill in "kidult" combinations of bright colors and border embroidery.

Trend:
embellishment

It was only natural. After several turgid years of black and beige minimalism and the basics that defined the look of the '90s, the fashion pendulum was destined to swing flamboyantly in the direction of everything and anything but basic. Dazzle for day—pieces with sequins, glass jewels, embroidery, and beading are now an expected part of the ready-to-wear landscape. Mixing embellished pieces with unadorned and simple shapes in wool, cotton, silk, or denim is the right balance for day-to-night dressing. A combination of decoration and lean proportions keeps things from looking overdone.

When the occasion calls for more than your little black dress and a few sparklers, and when nothing less than a knee-length knockout of a cocktail dress will do, take care: There is a fine line between divinely detailed and embellishment overload. In a style culture where women are encouraged by morning television fashion segments to look "red-carpet ready," the concept of real, understated, and (I hasten to add) appropriate glamour has become as muddled as the mint in a mojito.

Skimming and simple shapes rule the day for the Ageless Woman. Dark colors like midnight blue with black embellishments, for example, can transform a sheath or shift. However, all-over surface embellishment should be deliberately placed to cast very flattering shapes and shadows across your shape. The addition of one knockout, focal point accessory is enough to punctuate the look.

THE FOLLOWING PAGES ILLUSTRATE three different ways women wear each of these trends, and which of these approaches are aging and which is ageless.

▶ **Timeless:** The look of ageless personal style; up-to-date, clean-lined shapes; current proportions; a distinct absence of gimmicky details. A look that is chic and impervious to descriptions like young or old. Choosing good design (and perfecting the fit) is the key. This look is authentic, the real deal, and says, "I am comfortable in my skin."

▶ **Time's Up:** Looks that are adolescent; insistently girlish; a literal take on what the edgy young things are wearing; styles that look costumed and overly detailed; a too-faithful interpretation of a trend you are old enough to have worn the first time around; looks that are tight, short, and as subtle as a power saw. Wearing really young gear—when you are not—is a sartorial primal scream. Even though this stuff may have worked for you in the past, resist it now. The visual translation? "I am at war with myself."

▶ **At No Time:** Unflattering, oversized silhouettes; looks that are long past their expiration date; overwrought details, outfits as hypercoordinated as children's wear; pieces designed to look like "what the kids are wearing"; things like hokey motif or slogan tees; faux vintage jackets worn with pull-on pants; any look that squarely misses the mark. She may be plenty savvy and as engaging as it gets, but who would know when glancing at her on the street? Her look is on the outskirts of current fashion and announces, "I don't know and I just don't care anymore."

When women over 40 wear things that are too young or too matronly, they place themselves at a visual disadvantage. Their styles age them. Date them. Most critical, when looking at either approach, the first thing one thinks about is "how old is she anyway?" Keep in mind that the styling for the Timeless look for each trend is about sensibility: a pared-down simplicity and elegance. Refer to your edited shopping list in Chapter 3 and adapt the idea to your ideal shapes and proportions. Just as you will when you shop in real life.

So let's move on and look at some clothes.

Ageless:

- ▶ Wearing the right proportion jacket for your shape.
- ▶ A jacket of wool or cotton tweed with distinct surface texture and sophisticated color mixes.
- ▶ Couture details like hand-painted faux tweed; braid or fringe border trimmings.
- ▶ Unmatched-suit looks.
- ▶ Worn with jeans and flats (ideal for a casual workplace).
- ▶ Over a little black dress (another Chanel design first).
- ▶ A few Chanel-esque accessories per outfit.

Aging:

- ▶ Big shoulder pads and an oversized boxy shape.
- ▶ Wearing a matched suit with a dated silhouette.
- ▶ Wearing a matched suit in a girly candy color (very Elle Woods in *Legally Blond*).
- ▶ A jacket cropped above the waist worn with low-rise jeans and a tank or tee (muffin-top alert).
- ▶ Lots of accessories in one outfit; double C logos on your bag, shoes, sunglasses, jewelry.
- ▶ Heaps of cheap pearls and chains (cheeky and ironic for millennials; just plain cheap for us).

timeless

time's up

at no time

the little
tweed jacket

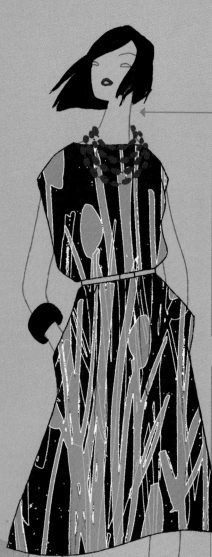

Ageless:

► Clear silhouettes; minimal details.
► Shirtwaists, wraps; shifts in abstracts.
► Avoiding anything that looks too literally retro in print and shape.
► Fabrics with hand-painted abstract florals.
► Prints of rich jewel tones; vegetable and mineral colors.
► Combinations of black, white, and gray.
► Blooms suited for city streets, offices.

Aging:

► Any Laura Ashley-esque garden prints; provincial, or otherwise quaint or sweet patterns.
► Prairie prints.
► Girly pastel prints.
► Mod "Youthquake" '60s florals (again, whoa! mind the irony).
► Palm Beach florals anywhere but very casual settings, resorts.
► Kidult clothes; any flower print that would look precious in a child's size.
► Florals worn anywhere but a garden party or a luau.

timeless

time's up

at no time

floral prints

Ageless:

- ▶ Wearing any truly classic and uncomplicated silhouette in an animal print (new and vintage), especially leopard.
- ▶ Leopard prints in colors other than the traditional browns, tans, and blacks.
- ▶ Wearing accessories with colors and textures that harmonize rather than compete with the graphic. Bolder is better here.
- ▶ Leopard accessories mixed with other patterns.
- ▶ Leopard print swimwear, sleepwear, lingerie.

Aging:

- ▶ Any baggy silhouette in an animal print.
- ▶ Wearing coordinated separates (especially with embroidered, beaded, or screen-printed motifs).
- ▶ Oversized intarsia sweaters with animals or animal faces.
- ▶ Leather or woven fabrics in a patchwork of many animal prints.
- ▶ A leopard bra or bustier worn as outerwear.
- ▶ Leopard that is short, tight, and shiny.
- ▶ Lots of ruffles, flounces, or tiers in any animal print.
- ▶ Wearing leopard clothing and leopard (or tiger, zebra, cheetah) accessories in the same outfit.
- ▶ Leopard-print gym wear.

timeless

time's up

at no time

animal prints

Ageless:

- ► A cardigan and knit skirt worn as an unmatched suit.
- ► Lightweight cardigan that subs for a blazer.
- ► Lightweight knit that subs for a blouse.
- ► Tailored, sweater-knit jackets and coats in cashmere, merino, or ponte.
- ► Geometric, tribal, multicolor patterns; flame stitches.
- ► Cashmere cardigan worn over an evening dress.

Aging:

- ► Knits that are short, tight, and clingy.
- ► Oversized, shapeless, baggy, and very boxy sweaters.
- ► Fishnet sweaters, tunics, or dresses.
- ► '50s-style short cardigans with nostalgic beading or embroidery.
- ► Fair Isle vests and crewnecks.
- ► Holiday sweaters.
- ► Fringe and/or pom-poms.
- ► Summer of Love crochet coats, vests, capes, ponchos.
- ► Crochet bikinis.

timeless

time's up

at no time

knits

Ageless:

► Pantsuits with classic lines.
► Jackets with nipped waists.
► Blazers and jackets inspired by equestrian/hunting/uniforms.
► French cuffs with silk knots.
► Men's silk foulard or striped scarves.
► Feminized versions of men's brogues and oxfords.
► Le Smoking–inspired tux jackets and pants.

Aging:

► The Gender Bender—a push-up bra or corset under a suit jacket.
► The Meet Cute—woman meets men's clothes, resulting in mountains of cleavage, cascades of hair (extensions), and a fedora (take note *American Idol* contestants, judges).
► Any menswear look worn by Carrie Bradshaw on *Sex and the City*. Fabulous character. Fabulous costuming. Unrealistic fashion role model.
► The Bermuda Triangle: Style void where proportion disappears; full pants hover at the ankle and jackets are too short to meet the top of a pant.
► Faux: Jackets with invented crests and insignias; a designer's monogram (sorry, don't care whose it is).

timeless

time's up

at no time

menswear

Ageless:

- ▶ Rows of brass buttons on a simple coat or jacket.
- ▶ Shirt dress, shirtwaist dress with military or safari styling.
- ▶ Cardigans, knit jackets, and coats with military styling.
- ▶ Sailor pants (Fit note: Fashion adapts the look regularly—in missy and plus sizes—so try a flattering trouser cut with mid- to wide-cut legs. A drop-front panel with vertical buttons creates a flattering camouflage for a full tummy.
- ▶ Safari jackets.
- ▶ French sailor jerseys.
- ▶ Berets.

Aging:

- ▶ Overembellished: trims, braids, buttons, emblems. Too much hardware, trimming, or braid and you "love a parade."
- ▶ Faux Army Navy looks found in the junior or contemporary departments.
- ▶ Oversized, shapeless pieces in fleece or washed cottons with army, navy, or safari details copied from younger markets for a "it's what the kids are wearing" look.
- ▶ Camouflage cargo pants.
- ▶ Takes on army or navy dress caps (alarmingly costumed).

timeless

time's up

at no time

military

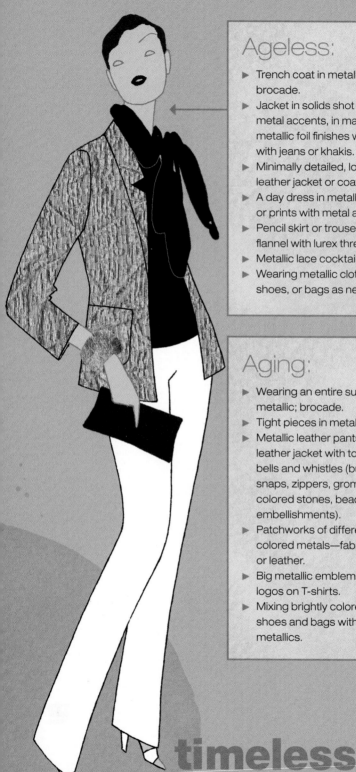

Ageless:

▶ Trench coat in metallic brocade.

▶ Jacket in solids shot with metal accents, in matelasse, metallic foil finishes worn with jeans or khakis.

▶ Minimally detailed, low-luster leather jacket or coat.

▶ A day dress in metallic silks or prints with metal accents.

▶ Pencil skirt or trousers in flannel with lurex threads.

▶ Metallic lace cocktail dress.

▶ Wearing metallic clothing, shoes, or bags as neutrals.

Aging:

▶ Wearing an entire suit of metallic; brocade.

▶ Tight pieces in metallics.

▶ Metallic leather pants, leather jacket with too many bells and whistles (buckles, snaps, zippers, grommets, colored stones, beaded embellishments).

▶ Patchworks of different colored metals—fabric or leather.

▶ Big metallic emblems and logos on T-shirts.

▶ Mixing brightly colored shoes and bags with metallics.

timeless

time's up

at no time

metallics

Ageless:

- ▶ The balance of combining classic Western tailoring with exotic printed pieces.
- ▶ Coats and jackets in unique ethnic prints to complete any simple outfit.
- ▶ Silk shirtwaist, wrap, or shift dress in an exotic pattern.
- ▶ Eclectic pattern mixes.
- ▶ Subtly dip-dyed clothes and accessories.
- ▶ Tunics with subtle beading or embroidery applied to a print.
- ▶ Silk pajama pants (for resorts/weekends).

Aging:

- ▶ Pieces with odd proportions: long shapeless skirts; short tops worn over baggy cropped pants; short vests over long tops; skirts that drag on the ground.
- ▶ Tie-dyed clothes and accessories.
- ▶ An overload of embellishments.
- ▶ Fringe, crochet, macrame.
- ▶ Limp cotton gauze or rayon prints.
- ▶ An ethnic print jeans jacket or jeans.
- ▶ Silk pajama pants with a matching motif shirt (worn everywhere).

timeless

time's up

at no time

global inspirations

Ageless:

- ▶ Tailored shirt in black or beige lace.
- ▶ A collarless topper, wrap, or trench coat in lace.
- ▶ Clean-lined jackets.
- ▶ Simple dress shapes like a shift, sheath, or an A-line in matte lace.
- ▶ Point d'appliqué—lace shapes applied to solid fabrics.
- ▶ Lace items in unexpected or muted colors.
- ▶ Little black dress with opaque black lace panels for shape.
- ▶ Blouse-length tunic top in lace worn over pants.

Aging:

- ▶ Ruffles and lace together in anything.
- ▶ Unlined shirts and tops (with bras).
- ▶ Macrame or crochet combined with lace.
- ▶ Tiered gypsy skirts in lace.
- ▶ Lace slip dresses in candy colors, baby nursery pastels, or white.
- ▶ Transparent (yep, your flesh as background) lace side panels in a dress.
- ▶ Blouse-length tunic top worn as a dress.

timeless

time's up

at no time

lace

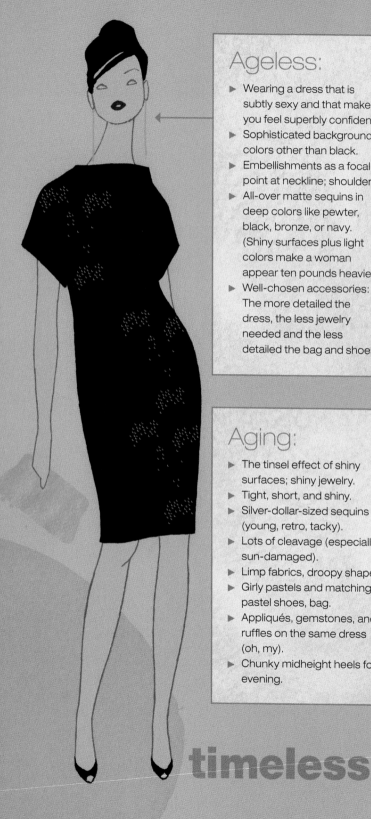

Ageless:

- ▶ Wearing a dress that is subtly sexy and that makes you feel superbly confident.
- ▶ Sophisticated background colors other than black.
- ▶ Embellishments as a focal point at neckline; shoulders.
- ▶ All-over matte sequins in deep colors like pewter, black, bronze, or navy. (Shiny surfaces plus light colors make a woman appear ten pounds heavier.)
- ▶ Well-chosen accessories: The more detailed the dress, the less jewelry needed and the less detailed the bag and shoes.

Aging:

- ▶ The tinsel effect of shiny surfaces; shiny jewelry.
- ▶ Tight, short, and shiny.
- ▶ Silver-dollar-sized sequins (young, retro, tacky).
- ▶ Lots of cleavage (especially sun-damaged).
- ▶ Limp fabrics, droopy shapes.
- ▶ Girly pastels and matching pastel shoes, bag.
- ▶ Appliqués, gemstones, and ruffles on the same dress (oh, my).
- ▶ Chunky midheight heels for evening.

timeless

time's up

at no time

embellishment

5 the illusionist

After years of styling all kinds of bodies for print photography and television commercials, I've learned more than a few things about dressing-room psychology. There isn't a woman alive, famous or not, who doesn't think (too much) about her perceived body flaws. Now, though, body image (and the illusion of perfection) is ratcheted up. Very young female celebrities represent the benchmark of the bodies we are encouraged to strive for in our 40s and 50s, and "midlife" celebrities like Demi Moore, Sharon Stone, and Madonna who are held up as "real" examples of how this is perfectly achievable with a little diligence, are completely unrealistic role models. Body perfection—whether attained through a rigid exercise regime like Madonna's or a combination of exercise and heavy-duty surgical intervention as reported of both Demi Moore and Sharon Stone (and anyone else over 40 in Hollywood)—is their business plan. Clearly, any woman who has a team of nutritionist, personal chef, trainer, cosmetic dermatologist, and plastic surgeon on speed dial can appear remarkably young for her age.

Visual reinvention does not necessitate procedures like liposuction, tummy tucks, or radical diets. You can rely on some alternatives. We all have features we choose to downplay and others we should learn to highlight. There are all kinds of clever and natural solutions that will lift your self-confidence along with your bustline. In underwear I trust. The right foundations make any woman feel more confident—instantly. More often than not, it's bad fit that adds years to a woman's appearance. This chapter is written as both a primer and a magic wand.

Every woman's style arsenal should include the right underpinnings for any outfit she wears in public. Your "wrapper," regardless of how carefully considered it may be, will not flatter your silhouette unless you wear the right underwear to support your shape. I am talking about pretty "utility" versus "dim the lights" lingerie: the worker-bee bras, line-smoothing stretch camisoles, budge-proof panties, tummy trimmers, bottom and thigh shapers, full and half-slips. The newest shapewear contours, controls, and slims every inch of the body from arms to ankles. It's easier than ever to wear what will lift, separate, and create symmetrical proportions under your clothing.

breast management

Let's start with bra fit, as no other garment establishes a more essential base for your overall silhouette. Whether your line is flattering or frumpy and aging depends on wearing the right bra for your shape and size. Along with your public wardrobe, your lingerie wardrobe should also evolve.

Many women arrive at a basic bra style and stay with it for decades. We ask our one style to step up and look great under anything from a T-shirt to an evening sheath. Ladies, it's time to diversify. To help me with this section I consulted with both Susan Nethero of {intimacy} stores (MyIntimacy.com) and Claire Brown, head buyer for figleaves.com.

Choosing a good bra is like choosing a good pair of shoes. Materials, comfort, and styling are better if you pay a bit more. In the thrall of fashion democracy, I've been swept off my feet a few times by the look and initial fit of private-label bras from some of the big discounters. Whether it was the band that seemed to stretch out overnight, the front closure that felt like a crab claw pinching my breastbone, or the seamless cup that developed cellulite after just a few hand washings, my good buys were short lived. Engineers have actually compared the construction of a quality bra to that of a suspension bridge. Think about it: an architectural masterpiece or a rope-walk under your sweater? Step up the quality. The more support you need, the more you will need to pay—$70 is a sensible average—for expert engineering along with lasting comfort and an impeccable line under your clothes. According to an independent study of five hundred bra-wearing women of all shapes and sizes conducted by {intimacy} stores, a woman's breasts will change shape, size, and distribution at least six times in her life due to changes like:

- Weight gain and loss
- Pregnancy, post-childbirth, and breastfeeding
- Hormones for birth control or hormone replacement therapy (HRT) that cause fluid retention
- Decreased physical activity
- Breast augmentation or reconstruction

Let's throw gravity in there too. Regardless of your size or shape, here is how your bra should fit, according to Susan Nethero. Toss any bra that does not:

▷ Provide a supportive structure for your breasts.
▷ Sit in the center of your torso. The cups should shape your breasts for a symmetrical look—making your torso appear longer and slimmer.
▷ Have a cup shape and depth that is in (exact) proportion with the size and shape of your breasts: This avoids spillage over the top or sides, or from the bottom of the cup, thus making you appear firmer and slimmer.
▷ Have the right strap width and length to prevent them from digging into or slipping off your shoulders. If your straps are pulled to the tightest setting, your bra is too big.
▷ The band fits securely across the middle of your back when fastened on the first (tightest) set of hooks (to accommodate a bit of stretching with wear). A band that rides up creates VBL (visible bra line: known less charitably as back bacon—that flesh roll above your band). Loose also means your breasts drift southward from lack of support.

Here are a few more fundamentals of bra fit I learned from Susan:

▷ Minimizer bras actually bind and compress breast tissue. (Yow! Isn't a mammogram enough compression for one year?) Compressed tissue loses firmness, and that causes droop—making you look thicker and heavier through the torso. A cup size should have the right depth to hold and lift your breasts—they will appear smaller and firmer rather than squeezed into submission.

▸ Underwire bras don't hurt or stand away from your rib cage if they fit properly. The wire should curve under and around your breast in a half-moon. The midpoint of the bra should lay flat and flush to your breastbone. For a bustline boost, underwire is your friend.

▸ Plunge cups should have a centerpiece no wider than one inch. Wider and it will cause the breasts to splay east and west.

▸ Seamed bras offer better lift and a more supportive structure than smooth cups. When fit properly the seams also provide nipple coverage. A good rule of thumb: Nipples should sit halfway between your shoulder and elbow. Horizontal seams are designed for optimal spacing and symmetry. Vertical seams are designed to distribute breast tissue for lift.

▸ A sports bra should not compress your breasts into a loaf-shaped unibreast. Neither should a bra allow breasts to thump up and down as you run on the treadmill. At any size, breast tissue needs the support of a construction with seams, shape, and cup depth to prevent impact damage to tissues and shoulder strain. Once tissues are damaged, they do not recover their original elasticity.

▸ Only wearing seamless bras is a bad idea. While they are essential for a smooth look under T-shirts and lightweight knits, a consistent diet of only these doesn't offer enough support. Alternate between seamless and seamed styles for less stress on your breast tissue.

▸ Wearing a strapless bra under anything but a strapless dress or top makes for a less than ideal shape under clothes. Without the vertical support of straps, slipping and pressure across the top of the cups causes what is known as banana boobs.

▸ Augmented breasts need the same support as natural breast tissue, sometimes a bit more depending on your skin's natural elasticity. Perky, droop-free breasts stay that way with a construction that supports breast tissue. The right support can prevent encapsulation and implant migration.

▸ After reconstructive surgery, ask for bras designed with a U-shaped underwire construction, which is deeper than traditional C-shaped underwires. Since silicone forms are often teardrop shaped, the U-wire is designed specifically to fit comfortably against the rib cage for the best support.

here's what is important to remember if you are going it on your own:

▸ Most professionals agree that the old formula of subtracting the measurement in inches of one's band size from the measurement in inches around her bust to arrive at her cup size is not reliable. Good bra fit always begins with the correct width band for your back. This is critical. The volume of your bust is contained in the cups; the band supports the structure. For instance, if you lose weight and your band width is reduced, this does not necessarily mean you need a smaller cup size. In fact, you may need a deeper/larger cup to properly fit the volume of your breasts. Nor does increased band size automatically mean a larger cup size. Your cup may stay the same.

▸ Visualize the shape and position of your breasts when you look at any cup. Where do they sit on your chest? Are they positioned south, east, and west? Have they lost volume and elasticity after nursing? Look at the shape of the cup, how deep or shallow it may be, and refer to the comprehensive bra checklist. Be sure that the cup provides the lift and symmetry you need—where you need it.

Undoubtedly you've heard that the best bra fit is achieved when you work with a professional fitter at a lingerie store. True. But let's say you shop at a department store (as we all do) and there isn't a trained salesperson in sight. Armed with your up-to-the-minute back measurement from Chapter 3 and the information above, you can put yourself in view of the right proportions and constructions—at any store.

It is economical in the long run to buy good-quality seamed styles along with a few smooth cups for T-shirts. Then use your top-shelf bras as a guide for finding good fit for less money. However, at discounters like Target, for example, smooth cup bras outnumber seamed styles. Why? Less engineering, lower price.

If a good specialty store is just not accessible, try online stores. Here there is a broader range of sizes and European designs (which historically offer more sophisticated engineering than our domestic brands). You can view what you need in your size and on a model rather than negotiating a snarl of bras on hangers. Online specialty stores like figleaves.com and herroom.com offer easy-to-navigate size finders that help eliminate guesswork. Wherever you buy them, always try your new bras on again at home under the clothes they are meant to complement before you commit and remove any tags.

tip   Wear your expensive new bras longer by hand-washing them in cold water and in a lingerie wash like Forever New. Commercial detergents break down the elastic in bras. Never but never put a bra in the dryer. The heat can crack the under-wire and will also wreak havoc on the elastic and break down the shape of molded cups.

the essential bra wardrobe for the ageless woman

Everyday Bras

Seamed styles that offer underwire support and proportionate shape: Have a few in your nude skin color. Seamed styles offer a more exact cup depth, which results in a round, natural appearance. Lacy textures pass muster only if they create a smooth surface under your top from 360 degrees.

tip   In your stylist's experience with breasts of many sizes and shapes, a universal success story is the balconette style. Try one for a nice shape and lift.

A and B cups:
- **Calvin Klein:** Perfectly Fit Mesh Lace Underwire Bra
- **Calvin Klein:** Perfectly Fit Balconette Push Up Bra
- **Donna Karan Intimates:** Stretch Lace 274 Bra
- **Freya:** Rio Underwire Balcony Bra
- **Huit:** Padded Lace Balconette Bra
- **Wacoal:** Embrace Lace Bra

C and D cups:
- **Cosabella:** Marlene Balconette Bra
- **Donna Karan Intimates:** Stretch Lace 274 Bra
- **Freya:** Darcey Underwire Balcony Bra
- **Le Mystère:** Tisha Bra in Lace 9955
- **Panache:** Superwire Tango Balconette Bra
- **Wacoal:** Stretch Lace Bra Style 6591

Deep cups:
- **Fantasie:** Anna Underwire Bra
- **Freya:** Phoebe Bra (to J cup)
- **Freya:** Darcey Underwire Balconnette Bra
- **Lane Bryant:** Cacique Lace Balconette Bra (to H Cup)
- **Le Mystère:** Tisha Bra in Lace 9955 (to G cup)
- **Panache:** Superbra Tango Underwire Balconnette Bra

Smooth Molded Cup Bras

Create the smoothest look under T-shirts and knits. A common misconception about molded cups is that they make breasts look bigger. Molded cups do not increase size. They create a rounder, centered, symmetrical-looking (and nipple-free) bustline. Fabric is laid over a metal bust cast and formed into a cup shape, sewn into the bra, and it can be either thin or transparent.

Suggestions for:

A and B cups:
- **Calvin Klein:** Perfectly Fit Naked T-shirt Bra
- **Chantelle:** Body Sculpt T-shirt Bra
- **Chantelle:** New Essensia Soft Cup T-shirt Bra
- **Le Mystère:** Tisha Seamless Molded Microfiber T-shirt Bra
- **Simone Perele:** Velia T-shirt Bra
- **Wacoal:** iBra

C and D cups:

- **Calvin Klein:** Perfectly Fit Naked T-shirt Bra
- **Chantelle:** New Essensia Underwire T-shirt Bra
- **Fantasie:** Smoothing Underwire Balcony T-shirt Bra
- **Le Mystère:** Renaissance Dream Tisha Smooth Cup Bra
- **Wacoal:** iContour T-shirt Bra
- **Va Bien:** Ultra-Lift Balconette T-shirt Bra

Deep cups:

- **Chantelle:** New Essensia Underwire T-shirt Bra (to F cup)
- **Chantelle:** Body Sculpt T-shirt Bra (to H cup)
- **Fantasie:** Smoothing Underwire Balcony T-shirt Bra
- **Lane Bryant:** Cacique Smooth Balconette Bra (to H cup)
- **Le Mystère:** Renaissance Dream Tisha Bra (to G cup)
- **Va Bien:** Ultra-Lift Balconette T-shirt Bra

Convertible Bras

To accommodate different necklines such as strapless, halter, one shoulder, and T-back dresses and tops. Your stylist suggests that these styles are necessary to buy only as needed. Shop with the dress or top in question to get the fit absolutely right. This is the best way to choose just the right cup shape, plunge, push-up and any other specifics needed to clinch the fit. Even when layered under a jacket, shrug, or wrap, there is no disguising droop or a lumpy bra line under revealing styles.

Suggestions for:

A to DD cups:

- **Dr. Robert Rey Convertible Strap Corset:** 5 star, no-slip fit that shapes and lifts

A and B cups:

- **Felina:** Hint of Skin Strapless Bra
- **Le Mystère:** Dream Shameless Strapless Bra
- **Wacoal:** Halo Lace Strapless Bra
- **Wonderbra:** Strapless Wonder Deep Plunge Bra

C and D cups:

- **Fantasie:** Allure Strapless Bra
- **Felina:** Hint of Skin Strapless Bra
- **Le Mystère:** Lolita Solutions Strapless Bra
- **Wacoal:** Halo Lace Strapless Bra

Deep cups:

- **Ballet:** Celebration Jasmine Multiway Bra
- **Fantasie:** Dream Molded Strapless Bra (to G cup)
- **Goddess:** Smooth Simplicity Bra (to DDD cup)
- **Lepel:** Athena Strapless Bra

Sports Bras

A good sports bra cuts down movement by 50 percent—important since the ligaments that support breast tissue can stretch significantly during exercise. Once they stretch, they don't recover, resulting in droop. Look for moisture-wicking fabrics and cushioned fastenings to avoid chafing.

tip This is the only bra that should ever go in the washing machine. Although line-drying makes them last longer, the average life of a good sports bra in heavy rotation is about one year.

Top-quality lines offered in a full range of sizes. Investigate and try on many styles to find your best fit:

- **Adidas by Stella McCartney**
- **Anita Active**
- **Bendon**
- **Champion**
- **Enell**
- **Lunaire**
- **Moving Comfort**
- **Shock Absorber**
- **Wacoal—CWX** (the Formula One of sports bras)

Shaping Low-neck Tanks and Tees

Layer one of these lightweight beauties under a T-shirt or lightweight knit:

- **Cass & Co.:** Invisibellas V-neck Tank—M/L, L/XL
- **Cass & Co.:** Three-quarter Sleeve Tee (arm shaping)
- **Commando:** TNK V-neck Tank (good for short waists)

- **Sassybax:** Torso Trim slims midriff, wireless knit-in support or underwire styles—S to 1X.
- **Yummie Tummie:** Freedom Tank has minimizing panels to smooth waistline from bust to hips, extra-long length to avoid ride-up. These provide anaconda strength control and take a little getting used to. You may find the results are worth it.
- **Yummie Tummie:** Crew and V-neck tees.

Improving Your Bottom Line

Ever wonder how some midlife ladies manage to look smooth and noticeably compact in their clothes—even when wearing thin fabrics like jersey or unlined stretch gabardine; or how voluptuous singers and actresses walk the red carpet or perform on stage looking so jiggle free? Here's how: They stock their lingerie drawers with budge-proof panties, shaping briefs, bike shorts, and bodysuits that lift and shape from breasts to midcalf—whatever is needed to create a line-free look.

Frou-Meets-Function Panties

They can be pretty and part of a mood-elevating bra and panty set, but they should also smooth over the tummy (leaving no visible belly balcony over the top of a too-low waistband) and fit snug under your bottom. Neither a cut that sits high on your cheeks nor one that rides up over said cheeks will cut it in this category. Finding "your pants" is no different from finding "your jeans"—try on several pairs. The waist should reach your navel if tummy control is the goal. If not, styles like stretch mesh or lace boy briefs and shorts that reach your high hip look saucy and smooth under clothes. It is worth it to spend a bit on a few expensive pairs. Fit and sensation count. Knowing how a great quality pair looks and feels makes it far easier to find good fit at lower prices.

Suggested brands for frou-and-function panties (and pretty sets):

- **Aubade**
- **Fayreform:** Pretty lace panels disguise tummy control.
- **Goddess:** Stretch lace with support.
- **Le Mystère:** No. 9 collection in particular.
- **Target:** Gilligan and O'Malley Lace Boy Shorts and Briefs (packs of three!). Buy them snug, as they stretch a bit.
- **Vanity Fair**

twenty-first-century breast etiquette

· ·

Along with It Bags and shoes, breasts have become a visible accessory unto themselves. No longer reserved for evening dresses, boobs on view are now as ubiquitous as jeans. As the '40s-era stripper Tilly the Tassle Twirler once advised her protégé, burlesque star Gypsy Rose Lee: "Don't dump the whole roast on a platter. Always leave them wanting more." In a low-cut, pushed-up, and breast-centric culture, how much of your cleavage is too much to display in public? Regardless of your age, what is your approach to style? Is it subtle or a bit more . . . flamboyant?

▷ **Work/Daytime:** Any cleavage reveal is too much, whether you are 55 or 25. A universal rule, regardless of your age: Never wear anything for day that dips below the middle of your breastbone.

▷ **Cocktail/Dinner Party:** Under-40s may wear things as low cut as the odd nipple grazer or get away with a navel plunger here and there, but for midlife ladies, particularly the well-endowed, necklines should rise one inch a decade. Does your poitrine communicate a sonic shriek for attention or leave more to the imagination? Like the lovely 50-something woman I met at a drinks party whose halter-sheathed bosoms left me with the sensation that I'd been chatting with two sagging cantaloupes. Ladies, one absolute truth about women with great personal style: They don't flaunt their cleavage in the face of the casual bystander.

▷ **Black Tie:** When a woman is over 40, the focal point of a formal dress is a beautiful neckline covering at least half of her chest. Too much "balcony" and you run the risk of looking blowzy.

▷ **Visible Lingerie:** Anything more than a whisper of lace from a neckline appears woefully obvious as a woman's need for affirmation that she is sexy. Which, of course, is always very un-sexy.

▷ **The Enhanced Bustline:** Many enhanced women clearly dress to showcase their newly minted breasts. If they find their breasts thrilling, who can blame them? But now that they've got them, Shock and Awe (Dolly Parton's names for hers) are no secret regardless of what they wear, so remember Tilly's advice: Better to cultivate an air of mystery.

State-of-the-Art Shaping

Line-free, seam-free, laser-cut panties in (your) nude are indispensable. Good under anything. These are among the best styles that I have tried in fittings (and stock in my own drawers).

Nude panties:

- **Barely There:** No Ride-Up Panties
- **Commando:** High-Waist Panty
- **Commando:** Boyshorts
- **Flexees:** Boyshorts
- **Jockey:** No Panty Line Promise (your stylist's favorite budge-free bargain pants)
- **Lane Bryant:** Cacique Wonderful Edge hi-leg brief
- **TC Fine Shapewear:** Just Enough Hi-Cut Shapewear Panty

Lower body shapers:

Bum lifting, tummy flattening, and thigh slimming; tugging on some of these gems from ankle to waist is a mini-workout in itself. Phew! The results, however, are worth it.

- **Avenue Body:** Seamless High-Waist Bike Short (to size 26)
- **Body Wrap:** High-Waist Capri Shaper—M–XL
- **Body Wrap:** Firm Control Brief
- **Cass & Co.:** Invisibellas Wear Repair Shaper Shorts
- **Dr. Rey:** High-Waist Step-In (support and shapng from rib cage to knees)
- **Grenier:** Sheer Control Lace (to midthigh)
- **LZ:** Microfiber Shaper—high waist to torso, leg ends above the knee
- **Sassybax:** Control Panty—sizes 2–16
- **Spanx:** Higher Power—high waist to torso, leg ends midthigh
- **Spanx:** Power Panties—midthigh, no leg band so no thigh bulge

Slips

A laser-cut full slip is ultra-lightweight and ideal under sheer dresses, tops, and skirts. Was your new skirt a great buy with a crappy lining? Cut the lining out and wear a laser-cut half-slip instead.

- **Cass & Co.:** Cami Dress
- **Commando:** Full and half styles; laser-cut edges, and weighted at the hem. Line-free and cling-free, skimming fit (your stylist's favorites from her kit bag and lingerie drawer).
- **Spanx:** Hide and Sleek in Full and Half-slips

Bodysuits

Your stylist's top choice for flawless, line-free shaping: the unitard. In my experience with voluptuous singers and actresses (also post-pregnancy, post–weight loss, post–plastic surgery) a shaping unitard is the line-free solution that moves with the body.

- **The Body Wrap:** Firm Control Suit
- **Lipo in a Box:** Capri Bodysuit has styles with and without underwire; shapes from breasts to midcalf—just brilliant for that long jersey or silk evening dress
- **Spanx:** Hide and Sleek Bodysuit
- **Spanx:** Slim Cognito Shaping Bodysuit

Hosiery

Hosiery is truly a generational issue. You may work in an office full of millenials who have never worn a pair of pantyhose in their lives and for whom bare legs are standard. The no-hosiery look remains a favorite of editors and designers who filed nude hose under "matronly" a decade ago. But the bare leg look requires a vein-free, sunspot-free finish.

Hosiery in a can: A makeup artist friend turned me on to Perfékt Body Perfection Gel (beauty.com) before I made a bare-legged personal appearance. This stuff smooths over my freckled and uneven skin tone like nothing else I have tried. I cover my stubborn spider veins and the fury of broken capillaries around my ankles with the Everything Pencil by Judith August, gently blending it with my fingers and off I go. This is as quick and easy as applying sheer foundation to my face and applying concealer to my undereye circles and bags. Other suggestions:

- Du Wop Revolution Tinted Body Moisturizer (sephora.com)
- Sally Hansen Airbrush Legs (drugstore.com)
- Scott Barnes Body Bling (beauty.com)

tip If you have the time, apply a good self-tanner for a day or two before a bare-legged week or a special occasion to create a more even base color. Try Mystic Spray Tan (sephora .com) or Strike Gold from True Blue Spa by Bath & Body Works (bathandbodyworks.com).

Nude stockings: Now, for the legions of women whose jobs take them to courtrooms, boardrooms, and high-powered conferences where bare legs do not look polished enough, here are some solutions. If sheer black stockings read as too dressy and it's nude stockings or nothing, these are the most natural looking:

- **Donna Karan:** The Nudes (available in plus and petite plus)
- **Donna Karan Hosiery:** The Ultimate Sheer Collection
- **Wolford-Le 9:** Pricey, but the finish is near invisible; flawless
- **Fogal:** 110 Noblesse
- **Bloomingdale's Silk Sensations:** Available in Women's sizes to 3X
- **Spanx:** All the Way Up High-Waist Pantyhose (available to size E)

Sheen: Keep it to a minimum in the daytime for the most natural (and modern) effect.

Textures and patterns: I must be honest. I have never been especially wild about textured stockings, period. Not even in the black fishnet and lace hosiery heyday of the '80s. On women of any age, textures have a way of devouring the focus of an outfit, not to mention that they can have a very thickening effect on calves and ankles. My suggestion: If you like the way your legs look in textures, have the legs of a greyhound, and thus want to create a focal point at your legs, wear a black textured leg like lace for cocktails to add surface interest to a simple black dress. Keep your look modern and avoid even a whiff of retro.

Opaque tights: Love 'em. My veins love them. Matte black tights are an ageless signifier of cool. With pumps, shoe booties, boots, and high-heeled sandals, nothing beats the leggy line of a black leg. Bright-colored tights move in and out of fashion, but one thing remains true: They are for kids. Go for colors like deep wine, indigo, eggplant, and dark brown to create rich tonal combinations with dresses, skirts, and shoes. Grown-up, individual, and gorgeous.

Swimwear

And now let's talk about the seasonal tug-of-war that is finding a swimsuit: I promise you, ladies, I have not delayed our discussion of swimsuits simply because the entire business of shopping for one can be so annoying. Swimsuits may be a torturous amalgam of lingerie, shapewear, and gymwear, but they are a necessary part of any ageless wardrobe that loves to swim and sun.

Here's how you will find your best fit:

▶ The shapes, proportions, and balance remedies that create your optimum silhouette in ready-to-wear should guide your swimsuit selections.

▶ Create a focal point at your shoulders and face with a flattering neckline and interesting upper body treatments.

▶ Take a cue from your best-fitting bra when choosing the cup construction in a bathing suit. Great bathing suit fit also starts with the right cup fit.

▶ Consider the fit of your favorite bodysuit or shaping briefs for how much you want to feel pulled in through your torso and abdomen.

▶ Use color to your advantage. Color is more important than ever. Walking half-naked in public speaks to the need for skin-flattering shades unlike any other "wrapper" you wear. You don't have to fall back on black.

▶ Don't rely on fluorescent lights alone. Always give a suit a test run at home (after a little self-tanning) in daylight. In front of your mirror, bend, stretch, sit down. Test the color against your skin. This is the only truly reliable way to look at the fit and the color. Do not snip those tags until you perform this little ritual. Do I need to mention "half-naked" again?

▶ Run through the "strategic placement" checklist (page 29) before you shop for a new suit.

Body types A and D look for:

- Necklines like sweetheart or halter that widen the appearance of shoulders. Treatments like decorative straps, color-blocked insets that draw the eye upward.
- Draping over the bust and torso for shaping.
- Colorblock combinations that are darker on the bottom.
- High-cut legs to minimize hips and thighs and lengthen the leg.
- Swimskirt styles that skim over your hips and upper thighs.
- For two piece or tankini styles, shop for individually sized separates for the best balance and fit.

Body types B and E look for:

- One-piece silhouettes with waist definition.
- Two-piece styles with underwire cups to lift your bustline for a longer, leaner-looking torso; a bottom constructed with a wide waistband to minimize a full tummy.
- V necklines, whether strapless, halter, or tank for a lengthening line.
- Strategic placement through the torso, waist, and hips like color blocking or diagonally placed pattern to emphasize an hourglass shape.

- Especially for tankinis—draping, shirring, or ruching to shape your midsection and highlight your waist.
- High-cut legs to minimize full hips and thighs.

Body types C and F look for:

- Empire tankini tops cut with an A-line to skim over a full torso and add width and a little curve at the high hip; bottoms with tummy control.
- One-piece styles with diagonal drape across the torso and over the hips for an hourglass look.
- Underwire bra constructions to lift your bustline for a longer, leaner-looking torso.
- Draping, shirring, or ruching or diagonally placed pattern to camouflage a full midsection.
- Two-piece and tankini styles, individually sized separates for the best balance and fit.

And finally, free and fail-safe: Stand up straight. No slumping or slouching. Your mother was right.

6 cherry-picking

The days of choosing from one or two designers for all of your wardrobe needs are long gone. Today, to look current and to create an individual, modern style, it's best to keep your eyes open wherever you shop and at every price, high to low. It's an item-by-item approach to keeping your wardrobe current. I call it cherry-picking, and it will help you learn how to navigate fashion's landmines—the extremes. For example, too much Juicy Couture and you're a parody of youth. A closet full of St. John and you're on a one-way ride to matron-town.

There is a misconception that a woman who dresses primarily in high fashion labels has the advantage of access to a sophisticated range of choice and thus has a far easier time looking "right" for her age. This is true only if she understands how to read the fine lines between youthful and too young. Have a stroll with me through the racks of Chloé or Gucci and I'll point out mid-40ish (and older) women buying very short dresses and skirts any day of the week. Money alone doesn't buy taste or judgment. What the designer area offers every woman—whether she ever shops there or not—is an opportunity to use high fashion as the source for ideas and details she'll spot else-where in various price ranges.

My point is that you should grow more comfortable with looking at things a piece at a time, rather than buying hypercoordinated looks from one or two lines or thinking that if something is found at the high fashion level it is always appropriate. Trawling through the racks of young-looking gear in contemporary departments, specialty stores, and discounters takes an especially keen eye to find a few gems. But they are there, and I'll take you on a virtual tour of the stores and explain how to spot what works and pass on what doesn't.

But before we go shopping, give some careful thought to every-thing we've talked about so far, specifically as it relates to your body type and your current wardrobe, and answer the following questions. First, make a list of the places you go in a typical month and next to each make a concise list of what you generally wear, then ask yourself:

- Is there a lot of repetition, and if so, what pieces do you wear most frequently?
- What colors and neutrals do you wear the most?
- How do you want to expand the selection?

How do you expand the selection?

- Upgrading the departments, stores, catalogues from which you generally shop?
- Updating the shapes?
- Upgrading the fabrics?
- Trying new colors, prints?

Are there many things that sit unworn in your closet? If so, what? And why?

- Make a short list of things you might pull to the front of your wardrobe and add into the mix.
- Make a list of those things you will never wear and why you won't.

Are you hanging on to things that are dated only because they fit you and "you never know when they might come back in style"? Make a short list of what you'd most like to edit from your wardrobe and to update in the same categories.

- If you are hanging on to coats and jackets from the '80s and early '90s with big shoulders and full arms, this is a tough tailoring job. Resetting a jacket arm is seldom successful and very expensive. These cannot be made current. Time to say so long.
- Do you have pieces in your wardrobe like dresses, special-looking blouses, or tops to pair with trousers or a skirt see you through a last-minute invitation after work or otherwise?
- Do you have a good tailor and do you improve the fit of your clothing with any needed alterations? Do you take advantage of stores that offer alterations for free?

So, imagine that you have hired me to overhaul your current wardrobe. It's scorched earth. You've leveled your closet, and while things are still smoldering, let's talk strategy. First, there are no magic bullets, no one-stop-shop collection or store or catalogue that will answer your every wardrobe need. Shopping—as we all do—at every price range and in all kinds of stores makes good sense, but you'll make informed, hipper-looking choices if you know what you are looking at. It's not necessary to pay stratospheric prices for great-looking clothes. A trained eye will serve you just as well as a bottomless bank account. A quality knockoff serves just as well as the source, but let's be clear—the woman who always seems to unearth an appropriate-looking fashion gem, whether she's rifling a designer sale rack or shopping at H&M or Zara, knows exactly what she wants to look like, knows exactly what kind of pieces she is after whenever she shops, and doesn't waste her time wandering a selling floor hoping that lightning will strike. She does some homework; she has a plan, and now so will you.

Let's start with research—and as I've mentioned before (a few times at this point), research starts at the top. The trick now is to pay attention to what's going on in high fashion—the paradigm of design. Quite simply, high fashion is the mother lode of pieces with cross-generational reach and the source of details we'll be looking at in varying price ranges. Modern-looking and well-designed clothes at any price have an ageless appeal. They stand on their own while leaving plenty of room for your particular self-expression.

In fashion's cosmos, the clothing collections found in department stores, from the good buys of the better department stores to the upper reaches of high fashion, are designed to provide us with two things: *fashion*—the new, the now, the knockout pieces, and what retail refers to as *wardrobing*. Of course wardrobing describes our workhorses; the solid-colored, good-quality, go-anywhere pieces that build outfits but are not exciting enough to throw on at the last minute and create a "look." The novelty printed coat, the metallic fabric skirt, the sweater with an embellished neck, the leopard print dress . . . fashion is what we are after now. Yes, it is important to keep those basics current so they work seamlessly with trendier pieces, but instead of buying more of the same, it's time to buy items that complete an outfit; pieces that stand on their own in your wardrobe whether you wear them with a pair of jeans or an evening skirt.

We all have a dream designer or two (or dozens). But the reality is that the vast majority of us do not shop at the high-fashion level. At least not exclusively. However, your stylist does encourage you to have a look at the real thing—if you want to interpret a Chanel jacket, then have a look at a real Chanel jacket. Along with the *shape, proportion,* and *fabric*—always the first three things to consider in anything you buy—note the subtle details that define the look: a fringed trim, a pocket piping, the width of a belt used at the waist, the sleeve length. When you look for your little tweed jacket along fashion's food chain, it's much easier to avoid the details that somehow get more noticeable the less expensive the garment, like the fringe trim that's transformed from understated to brushy, as if to scream, "Hey! Chanel detail here!!!"

Here's another suggestion: If you simply find the designer floor a bit intimidating or you have very limited time to shop, get online. Have a look at the runway collections of the designers you admire on sites like Style.com or Elle.com and take in the breadth of their collection. While every designer in the world now has his or her own Web site and many include their latest runway footage, the sites above offer one-stop, comprehensive A-to-Z access to what's happening.

And I'm not only looking at their current collections for what's in stores, but at their next season's collections as well. Like having your own crystal ball in your computer, looking ahead helps you avoid the built-in obsolescence of many shapes and obviously trendy details that you'll see in every magazine (and everywhere else) in rapid time. This is critical for shopping from lower-priced lines, specialty stores, and fast fashion. You want to spot the smart interpretation of a look or a detail and not the blunt force trauma in beads and trimmings. Take note of what silhouettes, shapes, and ideas move forward from one season to the next. This is how to choose a piece with legs.

Most important: It doesn't matter that the prices are positively jaw-dropping or that the sizing may not be right for you. Don't be distracted by the underfed teenagers wearing the clothes. Keep in mind that the simpler the clothes, the more over-the-top the styling may be, the more theatrical the hair and makeup will look to create the visual blast of young energy that spins fashion's wheels. Just concentrate on the clothes as they can relate to you and what you need.

Now think about the style profile(s) you most identified with in Chapter 1. Although from here on you are on your own to interpret things your way, those original profiles tell you a lot about your natural affinities for certain things. This is good. In the categories to come I'll

high-fashion cheat sheet

. . . .

(design features to look for in any price range)

Which pieces look streamlined, uncomplicated, and wearable enough for a chic and ageless look?

What shapes and details make classic tailoring look new?

What's happening with fabrics, colors, textures, and prints? (As we discussed in Chapter 4) Fabrics are critical. The simpler your shapes, the more that special-looking fabrics should expand the breadth of your wardrobe.

What's happening with embellishments, interesting shaped necklines, neckline treatments, and sleeve shapes and lengths that can work for you?

Which accessories can you easily add to a simple look to capture the new and now?

Which styles and cuts offer the right amount of coverage for you?

Is it youthful or too young?

call out which of the style profiles might benefit most from a particular sensibility. The point is not to abandon your personal preferences but to evolve them and to keep evolving them. Don't let your style grow static. Keep things moving by paying attention.

The lists below are an edited guide to launch your research and your shopping. A stylist is not doing her job if she merely grafts her own style onto her clients. You are developing a more discerning eye for what you like. I encourage you to avoid falling back on old habits and security blankets like buying more duplicate basics; instead put your money into one or two special pieces that elevate anything you wear them with. The idea now is to buy special, buy less, and buy better. Even if you can buy everything, don't just buy anything!

For the best of ageless style, here's how I categorize and conquer:

Vive la Femme: The designers at the ready-to-wear couture and designer sportswear levels that combine unabashedly feminine, couture-inspired details with precision tailoring. Fabrics are unique and luxurious. Take the time to study any of the designers below for the multigenerational appeal of their collections. Women in their 20s and in their 70s love these clothes. Something for every decade.

- Bill Blass
- Carolina Herrera
- Chanel
- Christian Dior
- J. Mendel
- Oscar de la Renta
- Valentino
- Versace
- Yves St. Laurent

Newer names in this category—same sensibility, slightly lower prices:

- Barbara Tfank
- Lela Rose
- Peter Som
- Rachel Roy
- Brian Reyes
- Talbot Runhof
- Tuleh
- Zac Posen

Style profiles: Matched, MCM, and Girly Girl in particular may find new ideas here.

The Modernists: Feminine shapes rendered with a minimalist hand. Streamlined chic. Architecture and line are the focus; clothes often have a sculptural quality and luxury fabrics take top billing over heavy embellishments. Have a look at the cross-generational lineup below:

- Alberta Ferretti
- Bottega Veneta
- Calvin Klein Collection
- **Chado Ralph Rucci:** Minimalist couture.
- **Donna Karan Collection:** The modern godmother of all things shape and drape.
- Fendi
- Giambatista Valli
- Jil Sander
- **Lanvin:** Sophistication, line, and femininity and the distinctly French je ne sais quois of mixing it all together with the grooviest embellishments. Everyone watches designer Alber Elbaz as his influence trickles down.
- **Narciso Rodriguez:** No one sculpts fabric better for a woman's curves. Deceptively simple looks with incredible constructions and fit.

- **Proenza Schouler:** Edgy press darlings who make beautifully tailored, hip clothes. Spot the ageless knockout items to mix or reference your way.
- **Stella McCartney:** Skews young, but her serious Savile Row training is always evident in her ageless-looking tailoring. The woman knows how to cut a pair of pants and a well-crafted jacket.

Newer names in this category:

- **Costelllo Tagliapietra:** Beautifully draped jersey dresses.
- **Devi Kroell:** This designer of exotic skin handbags and shoes has branched out into ready to wear.
- **Jasmin Santanen**
- **Jason Wu**
- **L'Wren Scott:** Sexy, urbane, a wee bit mannered, but the rock-and-roll intimations make sense—L'Wren Scott is Mick Jagger's girlfriend.
- **The Row (as in Savile Row):** Includes hip jersey knits and jackets. YSL and Rick Owens inspirations (among many). Sophisticated chic brought to you by the Olsen twins, who design the collection. No, I'm not kidding.
- **6267**
- **Yigal Azrouël**

The Eclectics: A mixed bag of designers known for extraordinary, often technologically innovative fabrics, unique color palettes and prints. Global inspirations abound. The multigenerational appeal of these lines is the source for all kinds of ageless looks and ideas. Miuccia Prada and Consuela Castiglione of Marni, both modern women in their 50s, design the pieces they want to wear themselves as they create new directions in fashion. Where they lead, others will follow in every hangtag bracket.

- **Andrew Gn:** Rich hippie inspirations.
- **Burberry Prorsum:** Seasonal reinventions of the iconic trench coat and sportswear classics inspired by all things English. Items interpreted in lovely fabrics like over-embroidered lace, metallics, and embellishments with a sharp and modern edge.
- **Dries Van Noten:** Exquisite textiles, hand embroidery, original prints; entirely elegant, cool, and ageless.
- **Etro:** Famous for their textiles of paisley, unique pattern and color, and opulent embellishments.
- **Jean-Paul Gaultier:** French couture meets French sailor meets African tribal decoration. All JPG inspirations.

- **Marni:** Intellectual, conceptual, but very wearable clothes for women who dress to please themselves. Men rarely understand these clothes.
- **Matthew Williamson:** Sexy, '70s, rich hippie vibe. Skews young.
- **Missoni:** Those signature flame-stitched knits mix with all kinds of looks.
- **Naeem Khan:** Elegant shapes and ethnic prints.
- **Oscar de la Renta:** His passion for Indian and African design is evident in his unique prints, patterns, and beading. You'll see Oscar's imprint everywhere from sportswear to dress lines.
- **Prada:** Multigenerational icon.
- **Roberto Cavalli:** Weed through the high-priced trash and flash to find truly great prints and boho chic.
- **Vera Wang:** Has evolved her designs from "pretty girl on a red carpet dressing" to a modernist meets artisan sensibility. Easy, elegant shapes. Moody color palette.

Newer names in this category:

- **Behnaz Sarafpour**
- **Michael Angel**
- **Peter Pilotto**
- **Thakoon**

All categories can find ideas here, particularly Overripe, Middlescent, Girly Girl, and Novelty and Status Addict.

An Eclectic Category unto Himself: Marc Jacobs Collection and his designs for Louis Vuitton ready-to-wear vary dramatically from season to season and will be as different in direction as the decade from which Mr. Jacobs has mined his current ideas. Both lines are worth a look for ideas. However, a caveat: The Marc Jacobs Look can play as self-consciously hip; no sparing the irony, and Louis Vuitton often reflects a more dressed-up-Parisian-inflected nod to same when worn in total. Over 40s should cherry-pick for individual items: jackets, coats, dresses, beautiful knits in particular. "The Look" often reads as too retro-referential on grown-up ladies over 40. All kinds of women respond to these clothes depending on where the collection is going in a season.

Modern Classics: Luxurious, clean-lined sportswear. And what's better than that?

- **Agnona**
- **Akris**
- **Aquascutum**

- Black Fleece by Brooks Brothers
- Brunello Cucinelli
- Burberry (the classic wardrobing pieces)
- Derek Lam for Tod's
- **Giorgio Armani:** Remains the go-to designer for corporate women everywhere.
- Hermès
- Loro Piana
- Michael Kors
- Piazza Sempione
- Ralph Lauren
- **Yves St. Laurent Edition 24:** Seasonless and sharply edited; a collection of wardrobe essentials day to evening; designed to pack and travel (at St. Laurent boutiques and select Neiman Marcus stores).

Everyone can find good ideas here. Whatever your style, mix it with classics!

The Futurists: Don't be thrown by the avant-garde edge on the runway. These designers are known for innovative constructions and beautiful tailoring; good ideas for those who prefer a minimalist approach. Focus on the close-cut jacket proportions. If you favor full pants or long skirts, these are the modern-looking proportions to buy or approximate.

- **Balenciaga:** One of fashion's most influential designers, Nicolas Ghesquiere, inventive, always ahead, widely interpreted.
- **Rick Owens:** Incredible jackets and coats; clean and spare sculpted leathers.
- **Yohji Yamamoto:** Jackets, pants, long skirts. The art-school girl—grown up.

Nineties Wardrobe and Middlescent, in particular, may find sophisticated updates here.

Zenwear: Easy, unstructured but never sloppy pieces. These lines are known for relaxed shapes that don't overwhelm the line of one's body.

- **DKNY Pure**
- **Dusan**
- **Eileen Fisher** (missy and plus)
- **Shirin Guild**
- **Yeohlee**

The Active Wearer in particular may find great upgrades here.

editing

Another thing to keep in mind: In many respects, your shopping experience can only be as good as the individual store's fashion direction and talent for editing their merchandise. That jam-packed look on many selling floors says it all. Marketers refer to the "individual style" phenomenon in fashion when trying to explain how one can see so many different trends grouped together for no apparent reason. I think it might be explained this way: As all things fashion and style have mushroomed from Western preoccupation to a global obsession with brands and hot trends, designers and retailers seem to reason that if they throw enough at the wall—short, long, loose, tight, narrow, wide, colorful, neutral, retro and embellished, minimal and unembellished—a few things are sure to stick. It's not so easy to tap into what has become a vast (and growing) maturing market. Women over 40 come in many shapes and sizes and our tastes swing from conservative to avant-garde, grown-up to arrested adolescence.

Decide what you are going for; be your own editor. Ultimately, no one can better understand how to put things together for your wardrobe than you.

Now, let's go shopping.

fashion and wardrobing for body types A, B, and C

Neo-Bridge

Let's walk the bridge floor. Or what was once known as the bridge floor. These are pieces with prices traditionally 50 percent less than designer. What are now known as contemporary bridge lines are designed to address the lifestyles of women who seldom wear suits to work or meetings and who blend their work and leisure wardrobes. Designers with their sights trained on high fashion at easier prices have reinvigorated what had become a moribund category. As you may have noticed, there is now an emphasis on youthful individual fashion items that stand on their own. The sensibility is more contemporary, featuring modern-looking and slimmer (but not skinny) fit rather than the shoulder-padded, boxy shapes of old-guard bridge/career designers such as Ellen Tracy.

In some stores you may find a few of the following collections in designer departments but most are found in the bridge department, and others in the contemporary department—it just depends on how a store divides its real estate:

- **Akris Punto:** Straddles designer sportswear and bridge.
- **Armani Collezioni:** Straddles designer and bridge.
- **Badgley Mischka Platinum:** Metallic brocades, feminine cuts and details. Nothing groundbreaking here, but worth a look for a Vive la Femme sensibility.
- **Barneys Private Label:** Offers fashion pieces with a slightly retro flavor in expensive and unique fabrics; wardrobing pieces to size 12 and 14. Standout novelty coats in luxe fabrics.
- **Boss Hugo Boss:** Sharply tailored and minimally styled wardrobing.
- **Burberry:** A more classic approach to fashion than the Brit edginess of designer-priced Prorsum. Great dresses, coats. Comb through.
- **Chaiken:** Known for their wonderful pant fit, the fashion quotient grows more sophisticated and designer looking every season.
- **Charles Nolan:** Ideas can be all over the map but the collection is well made and always feminine.
- **David Meister:** Dresses in particular.
- **DKNY:** A full range of hip, trends-aware pieces and the well-cut wardrobing that the collection is known for.
- **Elie Tahari:** A large, comprehensive selection in any season. Stick with the cleanest and most sophisticated of the fashion items—jackets, coats, great pants, and low-detail leather pieces. In other words, the very well-made wardrobing pieces they are known for. Give a wide berth to the profusion of too girly and faux vintage looks.
- **Galliano:** Spin-off items from John Galliano's RTW collections, a source for the couture-looking blouse to pair with tailoring. Vive la Femme!
- **Ginny H:** Tommy Hilfiger's sister designs a small, focused, and appealing assortment of modern-looking pieces. Nice fabrics.
- **Jon by Teri Jon:** A very Vive la Femme look. A good source for that little tweed jacket, shapely suits with couture details by Rickie Freeman for Teri Jon, and dresses under the same label. Look for all of these lines combined in one area in the bridge department.

- **Lafayette 148:** Eclectic details abound, lovely items, great fit. A solid and easy-to-wear collection that can fill in the gaps for all kinds of wardrobes.
- **M Missoni:** The flame-stitched status look of their top-tier line. Great pieces for urban and resort dressing alike.
- **Pink Tartan:** The fashion pieces generally include fun metallic brocade and interesting textures. Item driven.
- **Ports 1961:** Eclectic. Global inspirations abound. A collection filled with terrific fabrics and items. The simple and streamlined pieces can look truly great. Sidestep the tricky constructions.
- **Strenesse Gabriele Strehle:** Fashion pieces and trends-aware wardrobing.
- **tevrow+chase:** Cuts a mean trouser for fuller bottoms. The look is updated classic and the fit of skirts, jackets, and trenches is true to size. Good wardrobing pieces to mix high and low.
- **Tory Burch:** A global inspiration by way of Chestnut Hill and Palm Beach. A fun and colorful, early '70s country club vibe. Quality is top notch, but this line suffers from logo overload. The TB gold buttons, insignias on bags, on T-shirt fronts, jeans back pockets, TB scarf prints, and, of course, emblazoned on the (much-imitated) Reva ballet flat can all be too much of an already obvious thing. Talk about brand recognition. Clearly this logo mania is not hurting business, but ladies, let's all be a bit more individual than this. A woman should not see herself coming and going. Cherry-pick the lovely cardigans (and promptly change the buttons as your stylist does), easy dress shapes, colorful embellished pieces, and logo-free gear. It's all there and then some.
- **Valentino Red:** The same Vive la Femme spirit found in the couture- and designer-level designs trickles down to this small collection of very feminine items. Shapely, detailed knits and skirts are especially nice.

Old-Guard Bridge

- **Ellen Tracy:** Don't overlook the grande dame of career dressing. The quality has always been excellent and the company is focused on modernizing their shapes. The fit is full but sleek—providing you concentrate on finding the most updated shapes (especially for pants). Dresses are good, and they have always made luxe and classic lightweight coats.
- **Escada Sport:** Many of the ideas trickle down directly from top-of-the-line Escada.

Finding the Best of the Better Department

The go-to destination for affordable modern classics has had a few nips and tucks and could use a few more. Shapes are becoming more contemporary in combination with a realistic fit for women's bodies. This is the department for those comfortably priced and very anonymous separates that look right dressed down for casual offices. When you cannot bear the thought of paying hundreds of dollars for a pencil skirt or a pair of simple pants, this is the place to comb through for pieces that look good for less. Stick with neutrals, upgrade the buttons for a more designer look, and remember, plan to factor in a little extra for alterations if needed to clinch the fit.

- **AK Anne Klein:** Dresses are particularly good. Watch out for the heavy-handed coordination, however. It looks dated. Look for current wardrobing items.

- **Calvin Klein:** Something critical is lost in the translation between Calvin Klein Collection and CK Calvin Klein—fabric and fit. Unlike Calvin Klein Collection, where luxurious and unique fabrics and sharp shapes define the look, it is very hard to approximate that look with CK Calvin Klein's lower-quality fabrics. The fit is variable and the sewing can be shoddy. Colors are often drab. Worth a look if you have determined that the fit works for you, otherwise there are better options out there.

- **Jones New York Collection:** Offers their most modern proportions and trends-aware pieces. Quality is good. Your stylist often scores the odd on-the-down-low piece here.

- **Lauren Ralph Lauren:** Classic and often vintage Ralph Lauren inspirations. Fabrics are good for the price and the fit is true to size to a bit large. If you are a Lauren devotee, study the current top-tier and designer sportswear collections for crossover ideas. It's hard to go wrong mixing in clean classics. Two caveats: The crests and insignias and RL monograms are a "No" for an ageless look. These are free advertising for Ralph. The pant shapes are not consistently modern looking. Some legs are too wide through the thighs and then too narrow at the ankle. Pay attention here.

> tip The more familiar you are with top-of-the-line Ralph, the easier it is to spot the current-looking pieces here and there and then trickle down to the American Living collection at JCPenney.

- **Liz Claiborne:** An anchor in the better department since the early '80s, a new design direction will launch in spring 2009. Stay tuned.
- **Michael Michael Kors:** Needs more direct trickle-down from the Michael Kors designer collection. The styling of most of the separates is very good, and the ideas here are among the most modern on offer in this area to date. Stick with the most sophisticated pieces (namely the pieces that hew most closely to his expensive gear) for a chic, designer look. Jeans fit is also very flattering for tummies and fuller bums.
- **Tommy Hilfiger:** Exclusive to Macy's. The collection is a trends-aware mix filtered through Hilfiger's spin on preppy American classics. Certainly worth a look when you are out with your list at Macy's.

Contemporary Crossovers

This is a crowded field. Some contemporary floors look like the retail equivalent of a nervous breakdown. While still the destination for hundreds of niche denim lines and slogan tees, contemporary has rapidly expanded to include designers who have their eyes trained on a more sophisticated designer look. If contemporary fit works for you (and an item is not too girly or adolescent-looking) it is always worth a spin through the racks for trends at a lower price than bridge.

tip To maintain your sanity and keep your dignity intact in the fitting room, remember that the patterns here are made for a slim fit, shoulders and armholes are small and close fitting, hips are straight and narrow, and pant rises are lower. Size up one and sometimes two to find the right amount of ease. A touch of young in an outfit is fine, but young and tight cheapens the entire effect.

Who to try:
- **Diane von Furstenberg:** Usually found in the contemporary department. Always includes items with multigenerational appeal. DVF's signature wrap dresses are only part of the offerings in a season. Good fabrics, expensive looking, unique prints in lightweight coats

to wear over anything. 1970s St. Laurent and Oscar de la Renta frequently come to mind. Have a look at Diane herself. Gorgeous and in her 60s; dressed in her own designs, she is the personification of ageless, multigenerational chic.

- **Isli:** The line always features a few knit jackets in a season that work for ageless. Their signature sequin jackets are a fun and less expensive way to add an embellished piece to your wardrobe.
- **Nanette Lepore:** While this is quintessentially retro Girly Girl line, each season there are more pieces, such as the item blouse, special jacket, or coat that read more Vive la Femme designer.
- **Theory:** Most of us who have shopped Theory think of quality workhorse pieces. Most of the fashion pieces skew a bit young, but the clean-as-a-whistle leather jackets, coats, raincoats, toppers, and jackets look designer for contemporary prices. The pant fit is very slim and contemporary. Their stretch cotton shirts fit well but are overpriced. Wait for sales.
- **3.1 Phillip Lim:** Lots of ideas; the collection is filled with ageless pieces in any season. Coats and knits are particularly multigenerational. Tall women, have a look at 3.1 Phillip Lim menswear, too, for knits, jackets, and coats.
- **Tracy Reese:** Adds more couture-inspired sophistication and less Girly Girl to her collection with every season. Great-looking pants, embellished items, prints, color, fun. Fabrics and finishes are always nice.
- **Vera Wang Lavender Label:** Impressive quality for the price; proportions and details taken from her designer collection. Pay attention to the look here for more expensive looking details that have trickled down to her Simply Vera line at Kohl's.
- **Vince:** Casual, cool, and young, but there are always cross-generational knits that look great for the price. Stand-out, simple knit cardigans, sweater jackets. Nice lightweight and clean leather jackets and coats.

Accessible Specialty Stores

▶ **Ann Taylor** (stores and anntaylor.com): Stuck between the hyper-coordination of old-school career dressing and their attempts at more current fashion references. Somehow that embellished "Marni"-esque neckline looks odd on a blouse or dress silhouette that isn't current looking. They have always had a reliable pants fit and the wider leg cuts are the better bets. Their design direction is in transition. Until they catch up to their competition, have a look for those under-the-radar basics—pants, solid skirts, the long black holiday skirt paired with a great white shirt for an evening look straight from Carolina Herrera's playbook.

▹ **Ann Taylor Loft:** More contemporary shapes than big sister Ann, but the overall look is neither special nor is it especially sophisticated; quality and fit is all over the place, so factor in tailoring costs if you find a few things here and there. Essentially, these are young mommy clothes.

▹ **Banana Republic Monogram** (stores and online at bananarepub lic.com): Monogram, the smaller collection within the collection is distinguished by upgrades in sophistication, and fabrics like silks, wool and silk blends, and finer leathers; more refined details. High-fashion references and prices about 15 percent higher than Banana Republic's less expensive and reliable everygirl looks.

▹ **Club Monaco** (clubmonaco.com): Young, but there are the odd pieces for midlife ladies who can fit into their slim contemporary fit. Your stylist finds great sweaters, belts, scarves, basically bits and pieces that don't cost much and freshen things up here and there. Taller women can try the men's collection for cardigans and shirts that run longer while still slim cut.

▹ **Gap** (stores and gap.com): Current design direction puts Gap closer to the contemporary department than anywhere, but the fit is democratic and there are always ageless American classics to be found beyond the basics. The jeans area offers crystal-clear fit descriptions. Cotton sweaters, favorite-fit tees. You never know what useful thing you'll find. Special sizes available online.

▹ **J.Crew** (stores, catalogue, and online at jcrew.com): Along with an ageless staple—the well-priced cashmere sweater in great colors, don't overlook the Super 120s seasonless wool pieces. Favorite fit trousers offer a realistic missy fit. Jackets have a contemporary fit, but special sizes are available; Super 120s pencil skirts and dresses too. Seasonal riffs on wardrobing classics like blazers, classic cotton button-downs, peacoats, and car coats, all have an ageless appeal.

▶ **J.Crew Collection** (stores, catalogue, and online at jcrew.com) has emerged with some of the smartest and most spirited and colorful cross-generational gear at essentially bridge prices. Stand-out pieces in incredible fabrics from some of Italy's best mills. A sleek early '60s couture vibe that avoids a too-girly look with clean and sophisticated silhouettes. Color, embellishment, metallic washes, and jacquard, cashmeres, knit jackets, and an exceptional attention to details like expensive-looking buttons and trims; quality finishes (inside and out). Not a logo in sight, unless you count your monogram, which you can have embroidered on a number of things. You can be 25 or 65 and wear these clothes.

▶ **Old Navy** (stores and oldnavy.com): For midlife ladies, most reliable for bargains on activewear, jeans, and basics.

▶ **Talbots:** Yet another old-guard classic in a state of transition. Talbot's attempts at new fashion seldom look modern enough for the trained eye. As they continue to shake out the cobwebs and establish an updated design direction, you can rely on the little black dresses; scarf print dresses look modern classic and the quality is good; pants offer a reliable missy fit, and there are cuts that are current looking enough for my very hip mom, who swears by their wide-leg trousers for a fluid, tummy concealing cut. They offer a side zip, flat-front style from time to time that offers a smooth look under tunics and longer sweaters. My mother-in-law swears by the classic, stovepipe cuts she finds in petites.

Worth a Look

▶ **Karen Millen:** British specialty store worldwide with U.S. locations in New York; Boston; San Francisco; L.A.; Atlanta; Washington, D.C.; Short Hills, New Jersey. Filled with snappy English High Street items—coats and jackets in particular have trends references with ageless appeal, and you won't see yourself coming and going. Sizing to U.K. 16/U.S. 12. Bridge prices.

▶ **Reiss:** Another Brit High Street chain with locations worldwide but available only in New York, Boston, San Francisco, Atlanta, Washington, D.C., L.A., Short Hills, New Jersey, and Boca Raton, Fla. in the United States. Bridge pricing; sizing to U.K. 14/U.S. 10. Items, interesting accessories.

Indispensables—Knits, Shirts, and Jeans

Knits

- **Adrienne Vittadini**: Two newly relaunched collections in the bridge and better departments.
- **Agnona:** Deluxe modern classic.
- **Armand Diradourian:** Eclectic.
- **Barneys Private Label** (stores and barneys.com)
- **Bruno Manetti**
- **Isli:** Contemporary.
- **Loro Piana:** Modern classics.
- **Lutz & Patmos:** Unique shapes, beautiful quality.
- **Peruvian Connection** (peruvianconnection.com): The Nimbus pullover—an extra-long tissue-weight baby alpaca tee that is ideal for layering and travel. While the overall collection is eccentric and all over the place, keep a look out for the Missoni-esque, Etro-esque items that appear now and then.
- **Ports 1961**
- **Pringle of Scotland:** Reinvigorated by new designers, lots of modern choice.
- **Tse Cashmere:** A modernist favorite.
- **Tse Say:** Tse bridge line.
- **Vivre Selection Cashmeres** (vivre.com).
- **White + Warren:** Well priced, great quality.

Great Shirts

- **Anne Fontaine** (stores and annefontaine.com): Filled with her elegant white shirt varietals.
- **Herion** (vivre.com): Jackie Kennedy in the '70s vibe in retro scarf and tie prints, trim fit.
- **J.Crew:** Best cotton shirts for the price; special sizes online.
- **Lafayette 148:** A bit more dressed up; shapely; interesting details; wrap shirts.
- **Rebecca & Drew** (rebeccaanddrew.com): Custom shirts measured by your bra size. No more gapping for cup sizes up to 38DD. Shirt dresses, tops and pants too.
- **Thomas Pink** (stores and thomaspink.com): Classics and special sizes.
- **Van Aken Custom Shirts** (vanakencustom.com): Classic and perfectly fit custom shirts; white cotton tux front a standout.

Jeans

Premium: approximately $125.00 and up (many available in tall and petite)

- **AG—Adriano Goldschmied:** The Bergman and Mona wide leg styles (to size 32).
- **Blue House Drive:** Contemporary styling with a true, fuller missy cut available in high, medium, and low rises.
- **Cambio:** A range of styles and rises up to missy 16.
- **Christopher Blue:** Slightly below the navel rise, straight, bootcut and wide leg styles. The Madison is a classic five-pocket with stretch; Jake trouser is good.
- **DKNY:** The seasonal styles found in the DKNY bridge collection.
- **Joe's Jeans:** Contemporary but curve-friendly cuts—Muse wide leg is versatile.
- **Not Your Daughter's Jeans** (notyourdaughtersjeans.com): Tummy Tuck Stretch.
- **Paige Premium Denim** (paigepremiumdenim.com): Hollywood Hills and Laurel Canyon are sleek, easy fit up to 34-inch waist online; tall and petites online.
- **Saltworks (swjeans.com):** Monroe Street contoured waist high-rise trouser.
- **Red Engine** (SundanceCatalog.com): The Essex Jean (2 to 14).
- **Tory Burch** (toryburch.com): Tory Classic Jean with flare, sizes to 32 inches; very good fit.

Midprice to good buys: $99 or lower

- **Ann Taylor:** Jeans fit is reliable, washes vary, and the Lindsay jean and trouser cuts offer good fit for average sizes and petites.
- **J.Crew** (stores and j.crew.com): Bootcut and trouser-cut styles that fit slim through hips and easy on thighs and legs, clean-lined fit up to 33 inches online; tall and petite online.
- **Banana Republic** (stores and bananarepublic.com): Reliable, realistic fit with a modern classic look; tall and petite online.
- **Gap** (stores and gap.com): Has really worked out their fit—clear-to-read charts in all stores and easy to navigate online.
- **Old Navy** (stores and oldnavy.com): Sweetheart offers higher rise; tall and petite online.
- **Levi's** (levis.com): A range of styles, including classic 501s adapted for missy fit; tall and petite online.

fast fashion

Here is your stylist's thirty-second marketing profile of fast fashion chains:

They all structure their merchandise on a pyramid, placing the very best of what they sell at the top; less special things fill out the middle, while budget basics and teen clothes form the base.

This can make your shopping sharp and shiny. Look at whatever is labeled as "collection," "special collection"; or whenever you see a limited collaboration with a famous designer (known as a "capsule collection"), this is where to shop. The lower you go on the pyramid, the younger, more disposable, or more basic things become. And the more obviously cheap looking. Stay focused. Get in, get out, retain your sanity.

▶ **H&M:** The source of some very sophisticated translations of street and catwalk style; ideas and constructions are good for the price, but it takes a trained eye to sift through and find the fabrics that can pass muster. Designer collaborations with the likes of Karl Lagerfeld, Stella McCartney, and Roberto Cavalli have put them on the map all over the globe. Home of $49 skirts, pants that are well designed, and ultra current to mix successfully with more expensive things. You'll generally find their top-of-the-line stuff front and center, but with new merchandise arriving weekly things are quickly sold out or absorbed in the morass. If you find yourself in Europe, do not miss a stop into H&M's more sophisticated cousin COS (Collection of Style). Everything the ageless wardrobe needs, designed with a modernist approach and great prices. They have not opened in the United States yet. A plea to Stockholm— U.S. women are waiting.

- **Zara:** Has morphed from a reliable source for grown-up-looking knockoffs and well-made and affordable tailored gear into a straight-off-the-runway ultra-contemporary (translation: young) selection. The odd piece—generally jackets and coats—with cross-generational appeal may be found only after a thorough shakedown of the Zara Woman line.

- **Forever 21:** Young, fast, and shiny. Everything is shiny. Unless you have forged a pact with the devil and will remain Forever 21, this is now a forever no. Even for accessories. Sorry, I know some moms swear by things they find when shopping with their teenagers, but the look is for teens and early twenties and it is unapologetically, flammably cheap. This gear looks teenile on midlife ladies.

democracy—for all body types

Your stylist loves "masstige" and access for all to well-designed affordable luxuries in a wide range of sizes. Inexpensive clothes have never been better designed. There is a new attention to smart style, modern-looking silhouettes, and proportions that have changed the landscape. But ladies, there are no free lunches. Low cost means fabrics are inexpensive and sewing quality can vary wildly.

- Stick with democratic fabrics like cotton, denim, and silks. Go for matte surfaces and choose neutrals over brights, which can look mighty cheap.
- Inexpensive seams can look puckered, bunchy, or as if they are rolling inward.
- Expensive hems are smooth and flat; cheap hems can look heavy and thick, so pay for a professional press to smooth things out.
- Pay attention to how any print or pattern is matched at the seams.
- If a lining is bunchy or crooked, cut it out and wear a slip.
- The softer a fabric or leather looks on your body, the more supple the drape and the more expensive it will look.
- Visible stitching should be straight. Crooked or clumped stitches scream cheap. And replace cheap plastic buttons with ones of better quality.
- When you unearth a gem, factor in the cost of a little tailoring and a professional press to spiff up the overall finish.

When a girl is 21 she may get away with a few puckering seams, cheap buttons, and obviously cheap fabrics. Indulgent passersby who know the difference chalk it up to an entry-level salary and inexperience. We midlife ladies do not get a free pass on any of this stuff. We must know better and learn how to fake it (well) with low-priced gear.

▷ **Target** (stores and target.com): Pioneered great design at great prices. The GO International capsule collections with top designers skew very young. This is not to say that there are not simple lined, cross-generational finds to be had—just not many. Ruthless editing required. Their accessory collaborations with jewelry and handbag designers are more successful for finding ageless buys. Mossimo missy and plus sizes for T-shirts, skirts, and cotton frocks to throw over a bathing suit; Gilligan & O'Malley nude, laser-cut T-shirt bras; undies that knock off some of the saucier higher priced panties are nice cost-cutters in the lingerie drawer. Very good buys on C9 By Champion missy and plus sizes work-out gear. Voluptuous girls might have a look through Liz Lange for options. Target currently lacks the equivalent of their GO International designer collaborations with designers who create more sophisticated and cross-generational pieces in their lineups for both missy and plus sizes.

▷ **Kohl's** (stores and kohls.com): The only game in town here is Simply Vera Vera Wang. It skews young, but if you've looked at Vera Wang Collection and Lavender Label, there are ageless crossovers to be found: cardigans, simple tops with nice details, coats and skirts in novelty prints with a high-fashion point of view, and jeans that are worth a look. Sandals are comfortable but run big. Missy to size 16.

▷ **JCPenney** (stores and the most selection on jcpenney.com): Item by item. American Living offers Polo Ralph Lauren classics. Best to go for the neutrals; most updated shapes rather than the RL basics one sees everywhere; button-front shirts with feminine details, the plain, noncrested blazers, dresses, skirts, and jeans. Missy sizes to 16. East 5th missy and plus sizes, updated shapes, and a decent range of choice in little black dresses, modern-looking jackets, and skirt shapes. Look through Worthington as well for missy and plus sizes. Although this is a more classic-looking range, there are modern shapes here and there. In general, stick with neutrals and add tailoring and pressing to your budget. Nicole by Nicole Miller skews very young, but look through for the one ageless-looking shift dress or full skirts in her colorful prints. Wear with more expensive accessories to fake it.

▶ **Wal-Mart:** George ME by Marc Eisen is smartly designed, nicely finished, and mind-blowingly inexpensive for the quality. Item by item—dresses, skirts, and jackets. Missy and plus sizes.

fashion and wardrobing for body types D, E, and F

Shopping the women's market defines the need for the item-by-item approach. While there has been progress in the five years since I last did a heavy-duty scouring of the plus-size market for *The Pocket Stylist*, it is still inadequate to the needs of voluptuous ladies who want to look chic and ageless. To avoid what looks too contemporary or junior market (emblem tees, baby-doll tunics, and dresses) or too matronly (boxy, stiff, shapeless, coordinated) takes an eye. So let's have a look at your best options.

First, your shopping experience is expanded significantly when you shop online. This gives you access to good choice, exclusives with specific stores, and a range with greater sophistication. Neiman Marcus, Nordstrom, and Saks Salon Z offer the most comprehensive online shopping selections and each buys differently. Investigate them all to see what looks most like you. Here you will see those designer references surface. Pricing begins in the Bridge zone and moves to Better. Sales can be downright cheap!

Second, let me tell you a quick story about a boutique in my Brooklyn neighborhood. Lee Lee's Valise carries sizes 10 to 28 and the owner, Lisa Dolan, is the vanguard of a new breed of shop owners who take the direction of their new merchandise into their own hands. Fed up with the lack of sophisticated (but still well priced) and trends-aware choice between "too junior market and too matronly," Lisa started buying her own quality viscose and Lycra fabrics and collaborating directly with designers, tweaking a pattern just so; having clothing cut in her fabrics has produced a line of exclusives.

The point (besides the good news that you can find these gems online at leeleesvalise.com) is that it is smart to build a relationship with boutiques where you live and shop. Ask for what you don't see. Be vocal. This is how store buying gets better.

And finally, know that women's clothing lines found in department stores will always represent big manufacturers. They have the production resources and money to afford the real estate in department stores. While the names haven't changed, the shapes and proportions have. There is more chic, simple, and modern choice to be found.

The trick is to develop some key uniforms—find who cuts your ideal jersey dress, your modern ponte pencil skirt and pants, your ideal wrap shirt, and find your perfect-fitting jeans. They are out there. Focus and be ruthless. Shapes, fabric, and a killer fit is always the way to begin. Don't settle. If you don't see it, move on. The only way to let retailers and designers know—loud and clear—that they do not get it is to reject any merchandise that does not look current enough. Here are some good options:

Full-Fashioned Contemporary Bridge

- **Anna Scholz:** Anna is a British import whose collection is primarily found in boutiques in the United States. Look for her trends-aware body-skimming jersey dresses and tops, long knit pieces, and other separates with great details at saks.com in Salon Z, neimanmarcus.com, and leeleesvalise.com.
- **Anne Klein New York:** Top-of-the-line Anne includes modern fashion and wardrobing pieces.
- **Harari:** Items like silk jackets and tunics that have an exotic, eclectic flavor to mix your way with anything from jeans to black evening pants.
- **Johnny Was:** Novelty pieces, embroideries; cherry-pick the pieces for the most modern-looking shapes.
- **Lafayette 148:** Fashion and wardrobing; shapely and trends-aware, fabrics are top-notch.
- **Maiya:** Gorgeous silk pieces; shaped tunics and dresses.
- **Sandy Starkman:** Day dresses and skirts with a rich hippie feel, embellished novelty coats for day into evening.
- **Tadashi:** Evening tops and dresses, and jersey day dresses.

Classic Bridge

- **Eileen Fisher:** Knits with easy drape and a Zen appeal. Unstructured coats in ponte and melton, ponte pants.
- **Ellen Tracy:** Trousers that are cut very well, pencil skirts; quality wardrobing pieces.
- **Marina Rinaldi:** Produced by Max Mara in a full range from investment dressing to jeans.

Contemporary Crossovers

Current shapes and details, new and now items to mix your way. Some skew young, so go for the right coverage and focal points along with the look.

- **Alice & Trixie:** Up-to-the-minute items, chic lightweight coats, ponte LBDs, short trendy dresses to wear over pants day to evening.
- **Amanda Uprichard:** Tunics and dresses in great prints.
- **ECI:** Ombré silk peasant tops, dresses that always look current in a season.
- **Eliza J.:** Chic dresses in great prints; embellishments.
- **Live a Little:** Trendy novelty jackets—built for a sprint and not for the long distance.
- **Olivia Harper:** Very shapely jersey dresses and tops, items (leeleesvalise.com).

Better Lines

You will often spot the best of these lines on the department store Web sites listed below. While there are the one-off fashion pieces to be found, look through specifically for those good quality and anonymous wardrobing pieces that reference high fashion classics to combine with more remarkable layers, tops, and so forth. Most of these lines carry good dress options. A general caveat: Pay attention to the pant shapes to be sure the shapes look current enough. And remember to budget for the tailoring tweaks that are a must to refine your fit from okay to perfection.

- **AK Anne Klein Woman**
- **Bloomingdale's Sutton Studio:** Best selection at bloomingdales.com.
- **Calvin Klein**

- **INC International Concepts:** Macy's stores and macys.com
- **Jones New York Signature**
- **Jones New York Woman**
- **Karen Kane:** Worth a rummage through what is generally a pretty frumpy collection to find good shirts, long knit cardigans, easy shapes in pants and skirts. Step back from the "outfits."
- **Lauren Ralph Lauren:** Outerwear and knits that sub as jackets; coats are worth a look. Skip the insignias or logos.
- **Liz Claiborne:** New design direction is intent on bringing Liz back to its Liz Claiborne–designed days and affordable chic heyday.
- **Michael Michael Kors:** Best designer-looking range in this market. Go for the chic pieces that most closely reference what he's doing in his designer collection in a season. Fit is generally true to size and flattering.

Dresses

Shapely and current in jersey and other fabrics:

- **Anna Scholz**
- **Calvin Klein:** LBDs in ponte, knits, and jersey.
- **Donna Ricco:** Styles for day and night.
- **Igigi:** Boutiques and igigi.com.
- **Lewis Cho:** Chic shifts.
- **Marina Rinaldi:** Modern classic dresses are always a part of their range.
- **Melissa Massi:** Good quality, curvy, draped jersey.
- **Monik by Charles Chang Lima:** Sizes 12 to 20 at select Saks.
- **Norma Kamali Timeless:** Exclusive to spiegel.com.
- **Olivia Harper:** Great short and long looks (leeleesvalise.com).
- **Rachel Pally White Label:** Some of the grooviest jersey dresses—short and long—in this market.
- **Tadashi:** Day and night.
- **Tennille White:** Draping, curvy jersey.

Coats

Lines with Contemporary Silhouettes:

- **Calvin Klein:** Better
- **Cinzia Rocca:** Bridge
- **DKNY:** Better

- **Ellen Tracy:** Bridge
- **Gallery:** Bridge
- **Hilary Radley:** Better to bridge; great raincoats to dressed shearlings
- **Marina Rinaldi:** Bridge to designer

Indispensables—Knits, Shirts, Jeans

Knits

- **C.enne.V**
- **Eileen Fisher:** Every collection has varying lengths in cardigans that work with just about anyone's style and any wardrobe.
- **Joan Vass**
- **Magaschoni**
- **Roni Rabl**

Shirts

Voluptuous girls look wonderful in shapely shirts—keep your eyes open everywhere for current details. A few standouts:

- **Gayla Bentley**
- **INC. at Macy's:** Quality not great, but they often have shirts with a look.
- **Karen Kane:** Shirt with a kimono tie for the waist; nice shape.
- **Lafayette 148:** Wrap shirts, waist ties, sleeve treatments.
- **Lane Bryant:** Corset stitching and other waist treatments, shoulder tucks; fabric okay.
- **Talbot's Woman:** Updated sleeve treatments, classic, good fit and fabrics.

Jeans

Premium Denim: About $125 and higher

- **James Jeans** (stores and saks.com): Bootcut and straight leg to 24W; exclusive to Saks Salon Z.
- **Not Your Daughter's Jeans** (nordstrom.com): Various styles and a good selection in regular and tall.
- **Paige Premium Denim** (paigepremiumdenim.com): Topanga Wide legs and Augora Hils boot cuts to 24W.
- **Svoboda** (svobodastyle.com): The Eleanor is a classic shaped bootcut; Kate wide leg trouser dresses up well.

$99 and less

- **Avenue** (avenue.com): Classic five-pocket bootcut by Seven, nice fit.
- **Banana Republic** (stores and bananarepublic.com): Reliable, realistic fit with a modern classic look, to missy 16 online; tall and petite online.
- **Gap** (stores and gap.com): Has really worked out their fit—clear to read charts in all stores and fantastically efficient and easy to navigate online; many styles from which to find your best fit to 20/XXL; tall and petite online.
- **Lane Bryant** (lanebryant.com): Seven brand bootcuts and trousers, Right Fit Denim in Lafayette and Houston; Secret Slimmer offers a range of fit for average, tall, and petite.
- **Old Navy** (stores and oldnavy.com): The Sweetheart style offers a high rise to size 20; tall and petite in stores and online.

online shopping sites for all

Online shopping—A, B, and C

One-Stop Shopping

Access to the world of fashion online; lesser known brands, private labels, exclusives, and big brands alike. (Always check for sales.)

- **Barneys.com**
- **Bergdorfgoodman.com:** Great editing
- **Bloomingdales.com**
- **Neimanmarcus.com:** Great editing
- **Nordstrom.com:** Great editing
- **Macys.com**
- **Saks.com**

More Sites

- **Activeendeavors.com:** Young designers and groovy accessories amid trendy denim lines.
- **Eluxury.com:** Access to LVMH stable of RTW and accessories and more.
- **Intermixonline.com:** Items and accessories.
- **Kirnazabete.com:** Hard to find designers and accessories; a tightly edited selection online.

- **Net-a-porter.com:** Luxury designers and accessories; an exquisitely curated selection
- **Scoopnyc.com:** Items and accessories.
- **Shopbop.com:** Owned by Amazon.com; huge and all over the map, but this is the everywoman site.
- **Vivre.com:** The ultimate in cross-generational cool; broad price range from luxury to bridge and better pricing for clothes you will not see everywhere; exclusive pieces developed for Vivre collection; unusual accessories; great service; great sales.
- **Zappos.com**

Online shopping—D, E, and F

One-Stop Shopping

- **Bloomingdales.com:** Best selection of plus-sized and Sutton Studio knits are very good.
- **Neimanmarcus.com**
- **Nordstrom.com**
- **Macys.com:** A good selection of better merchandise
- **Saks.com:** For Salon Z.

More Sites

- **14to24w.com:** A discounter of designer merchandise from Eileen Fisher, Ellen Tracy, Harari, and more.
- **Abbyz.com**
- **Alight.com**
- **Igigi.com**
- **Kiyonna.com:** Contemporary items to cherry-pick; a caveat: Fit is erratic.
- **Leeleesvalise.com:** A true boutique experience online; personal questions answered easily.
- **Trentacosta.com:** For styles from Darren Trentacosta; also in specialty stores. Simply great sophisticated fashion and wardrobing pieces. Current and clean shapes, nice details.
- **Truejeans.com**
- **Spiegel.com:** Cherry-pick the Signature Collection for missy sizes 18 to 20.
- **Talbots.com:** Pants fit well; simple dress shapes; nice shirts; but work your way around all the matronly, dated-looking merchandise and go for anonymous wardrobing.
- **Zafu.com**

always ageless buys

Jackets and Coats

- At least one tailored jacket (that fits to the teeth).
- Little tweed jacket.
- Black tuxedo jacket—inspired by YSL's Le Smoking.
- Unadorned leather jacket: an anchor piece for high/low dressing. In black—only a wink at motorcycle; mind the snaps and zippers.
- Tailored daytime coat in a bright color (to boost the neutrals underneath).
- Weekend coat: Cotton twill, wool, oilcloth, in an au courant shape.
- Trench coat: Reliable tan cotton; leopard; metallic.
- Novelty jacket: Distinctive fabric and a modern proportion (buy or resurrect a quality vintage piece).
- Novelty coat: A print; a graphic, floral, or an embellished fabric.
- Metallic jacket or coat for day-to-evening.
- Peacoat.

Dresses

- Shirtwaist.
- Sheath.
- A-line.
- Tunic.
- Wrap dress: Any fabric, but have one in matte wool or silk viscose jersey.
- Any of the above in black, leopard print, global-inspired prints, graphic floral, art prints with metallic accents.

Shirts and Tops

- The simple white shirt—day and evening.
- The dressed-up shirt.
- Tuxedo-pleated fronts.
- Silk button-front in leopard.
- Silk chiffon blouse.
- French sailor top.

Knits

- Cashmere V-front cardigans in black and off-white.
- Patterned cardigan (think Missoni).
- Solid cashmere sweaters in a few statement colors.
- Leopard twinset.
- A sweater with an embellished neckline or cuffs (or both).
- Sturdy weekend cardigan.
- Tissue-weight wool shrug—the love child of the shawl and the sweater; kimono sleeves and soft drape to cover bare arms.

Bottoms

- Seasonless wool trousers in black, camel, ivory (have a pair that matches that tailored jacket with the killer fit as described above—read suit).
- Tuxedo or black pants (that work with a tuxedo jacket, naturally).
- Trouser-cut dark indigo jeans.
- Simple 5-pocket jeans in dark indigo and white.
- At least one seasonless wool skirt in your best shape(s).

for all: shop to save

Take advantage of discounters and Web sites that list discount shopping codes for a variety of online fashion sites; savings of 10 to 25 percent.

- **Bluefly.com:** One of the first and still one of the best for deals.
- **Dealhunting.com:** For online discount codes.
- **Dealtime.com:** Enter what you want and they search prices from a huge pool of retailers.
- **Mysimon.com:** Same as above; tell them what you want and they do the Web search.
- **Reesycakes:** For codes.
- **Shopfrankeys.com:** For codes.
- **Shopittome.com:** Tell them what you want and they send you e-mail alerts about sales at places like Bloomingdale's, Nordstrom, and Saks.
- **Toutie.com:** For codes.

7 accessories

"It's all in the mix": An idea and instruction that's tossed off regularly by magazines and tele-fashionists. And while we all understand that "the mix" refers to our preferred combinations of expensive things worn with less expensive gear and bargains, what is never clearly pinned down is how one refines the mix for an ageless look. Your stylist believes it is the discriminating and unexpected combination of trends and tailoring—mixing old favorites with fashion's latest interpretations of the same themes for a look that adds up to sophisticated, personal, and relevant.

Nothing pulls the mix together faster than good-looking and "now" accessories. The simpler our clothing shapes, the more we rely on the visual interest: the color, shine, and texture created by a mix of jewelry, bag, shoes, and eyeglasses into our everyday look. Every single thing you wear—every detail—conducts an ongoing monologue about you. Captivate your audience with accessories as intriguing and individualistic as you are.

jewelry

Ah, jewelry. Tactile, shiny, colorful—from earliest civilization women have adorned their bodies with jewelry as a visual statement of their identity. And so it is in the twenty-first century. The most direct glimpse into a woman's personality—at any age—is seen through her choice of jewelry.

In our teens and 20s jewelry is all fashion—a collection of signs, badges, and talismans that tell the world who we are (or who we want to be that week). Then, gradually, jewelry becomes about a woman's personal style and status and less—if at all—about fashion. The scale of individual pieces, the unique or conventional quality of her choices, her mix of colors, metals, stones, current styles with senti-mental pieces, expensive and not expensive—all of it tells her story.

Here is as close to an absolute truth as we can get: The jewelry a female wears and how she wears it separates the women from the girls, stylistically speaking. Always has and always will. Jewelry, in particu-lar (and accessories in general), is where many women wear things that blow their look entirely. A certain way to look more plugged-in and, yes, ageless, is to understand how to wear bolder, newer, gutsier things and still look like yourself.

So what distinguishes the look of the Ageless Woman's jewelry mix from, say, the woman who confuses wearing loads of cheap plastic and tinsel-toned pieces from Forever 21 and Mango for a young-looking edge? Or from the woman wearing a nameplate necklace announcing "World's Greatest Grandma" as a timeless everyday piece? (She may well be, but it's best not to confuse this brand of status with personal style.) Here is what Ageless knows about jewelry:

▷ She never wears things that look gimmicky, cheap, or dispos-able. She knows that anything that does will drag her look down entirely. She is very discriminating. One part of her style quotient is that whether she is wearing a stack of wooden bangles from an African market or très cher cuffs of exotic wood and diamonds from a big designer, she will wear them with the same regard. Whether real or faux, the look of her jewelry adds a significant style boost to anything she wears. Her things always read as good quality (what-ever they actually cost).

▷ Ageless has a keen eye and antenna for social currents and fashion trends alike. This is seen clearly by the way she mixes her jewelry. She pays attention to the new—just as she does with her clothes—but knows that with jewelry there is no easier way to experiment with a trend, try new looks, or wear new color accents. All these things will animate the clean lines and shapes of her wardrobe. She'll wear a piece of new with pieces from ten years ago, or vin-tage, or heirloom. Doesn't matter as long as she feels that the mix looks like her.

▷ Ageless wears things with a timeless cool that transcends her age; her mix has a certain détaché, or undone, quality that does not take itself too seriously—which always reads as youthful.

Why Faux Is Fab

For an instant, ageless style update, invest in a boffo statement piece of the best quality costume jewelry—new or vintage—that you can afford. Costume is experiencing a renaissance. Established and new designers alike are producing pieces with the kind of artistry found in the American costume jewelry making of the '40s and '50s. Spurred by the unique and boldly scaled runway pieces at Lanvin, Louis Vuitton, Chanel, and St. Laurent in particular, the jewelry industry has been quick to react. More fine jewelry designers are creating lower priced costume lines. Many costume jewelry designers are raising the quality of their materials and are now offering pieces made with the same techniques, mountings, and settings as fine jewelry; with combinations of materials like high-quality crystal "gems," glass stones and beads; and with a mixture of semiprecious stones, faux materials and high quality metal plating. Far from disposable, you won't find many of these things on the spinning carousels in most department stores. They are unique and many are glass-case items.

Why Bigger Is Better

Wearing a bold statement necklace is one of the best ways to experiment with a new trend or with new color combinations you might never buy in ready-to-wear or with a bigger scale (in proportion to you, of course) than you may have worn before. Bib-style necklaces draw the eye down from the neck (if it is a sensitivity) and cover the chest to the collarbone. Multi-strand styles like a Sautoir—multiple-strands of beads caught up with a pendant or ornamental closure—worn at just above or just below the breast create a textured and lengthening vertical focal point.

▶ Oversized brooches come in and out of fashion. For pure style and doing your own thing, they are one of the best instant focal points you can wear. Keep the look modern with a combination of pins—new or vintage or both—on a jacket or the front of a simple collarless coat, for example. Wear a big stone brooch over the clasp of oversized costume pearls. Pin a brooch or two on a satin scarf or cummerbund worn at your waist.

- Big cuffs stacked on a wrist (for tall and voluptuous ladies) or worn one on each wrist (for all) is a timeless and dynamic look. Fashion legend Diana Vreeland was seldom seen without her favorite pair of enameled black "Coco" cuffs emblazoned with the Maltese cross. Hers were by Kenneth Jay Lane, who has produced his faithful copies of the original Chanel design for decades.

- Long drop earrings and oversized evening dazzlers can be on your list, but with a few caveats: If your earring reaches your jawbone, be sure you want to create a focal point there. Ditto your neck. And remember, the bigger your earrings, the more intense the focus on just your face. All fine as long as you ultimately feel confident. Gargantuan saucer-sized drops, huge or very long earrings of lacy beadwork, and those multi-tiered chandeliers with an early '60s vibe are best worn by les jeunes filles.

- The great big right-hand ring. For day, try combinations of metal or enamel, wood, faux ivory, coral or turquoise, bone, or semiprecious or glass stones. Anything that will make your hand gestures look more intriguing and expressive. For cocktail rings, look for unusual materials—extra-large semiprecious stones, ground stones like pyrite that resemble old mashed-up rhinestones and colored glass stones combined with rhinestones will always look dazzling and fun.

Costume jewelry, either on its own or mixed with fine jewelry, will always express an attitude that is both ageless and individualistic. No one understood this better than Coco Chanel; she is also considered the architect of modern fashion costume jewelry. She innately understood that costume jewelry (hers was inspired by the lavish combinations of pearls and gems worn by Russian nobility) would give her simple shapes and casual fabrics a sense of cool without a hint of the jolie madame who wore the family jewels for day. Her collaborations with Fulco Verdura in the '30s produced the pieces women still covet today: ropes of glass pearls, chains with colored stones, whimsical, oversized brooches, and bold enameled cuffs with "gemstones." Wearing only real rocks, especially during the day, can look matronly (if not a bit eager to impress). Remember, it's all in that high and low, very personal mix.

Wearing a statement piece or two is a chic less-is-more strategy. Frankly, mature women look a little tentative in messy combinations of diminutive and girly jewelry with tiny charms, teensy pearls, and weensy gemstones on wispy little chains. Most of this stuff looks like a good sneeze could blow it away. What we want now is presence. One important piece creates that sophisticated-looking focal point that elevates anything you wear.

So let's talk about the trends that resurface and recycle in a near constant rotation. Chances are you have items in many of these categories in your jewelry box. Consider any and all of these trends as you choose the new:

Pearls (of course)

Forget the image of a dowager in a twinset—pearls can be dressy, sexy, offhandedly cool and chic, and work with all kinds of outfits.

A real strand of pearls is apt to be a graduated strand and a tidy collar length (at your throat), a choker (base of your neck), a princess (collarbone length), or a matinee (sits just above your chest). Dainty and real choker or collar-length pearls are for weddings, funerals, and passing down to the next generation. And those princess and matinee lengths will look less Midcentury Matron or Madame Secretary if you introduce them to very casual fabrics or tuck them inside the V of your white shirt or the neck of your T-shirt or V-neck sweater.

Now, our pearls should be larger, longer, all one size, and unapologetically fake. Alber Elbaz at Lanvin started the fashion of pearls strung loosely on ribbon. Like Chanel before him, he reinvented a classic by knocking the stuffy out of the look. Try on an opera or rope length (48 to 120 inches long) wrapped twice around your neck. Chanel said that "a woman should wear ropes and ropes of pearls."

There are so many impressive fakes to be had—new or vintage. The nicest faux pearls, like Chanel's, are still made as the Romans made them, by coating glass beads with mother of pearl. Other good fakes have a lovely iridescence that imitates the nacre on real pearls created by coating glass beads in Essence d'Orient, a fish-scale solution that looks better than it smells.

Mix larger-scale spherical (round) cultured pearls with Baroque (irregular, naturally shaped pearls). Choose the right white, ivory, or cream for your skin tone for a luminous look. Wear the deep gray tones that imitate Tahitian pearls if the color suits you. And don't overlook vintage strands. "Vintage faux pearls have a weight in the hand and a luster that you simply don't see as much in new styles," says Melody Rodgers, who sells a lot of them at her namesake store in New York City. "They are a great investment," she adds.

tip There are a few musts to know when buying vintage costume pearls, says Melody:

- Look closely at the individual beads. You want to be sure that color and luster are evenly distributed. If you find a few pearls that are worn or discolored (perfume is usually the culprit), don't pass on a strand in otherwise good condition.
- Always have vintage pearls restrung before you wear them—here is your chance to toss any discolored beads.
- Glass beads are the most lustrous and realistic looking.

Suggested Designers:

- **Carolee**
- **Carolee Luxe**
- **Chanel (naturally)**
- **Erickson Beamon**
- **Erwin Pearl**
- **Gerard Yosca**
- **Lanvin**
- **Lee Angel**
- **Miriam Haskell**
- **Natalia Brilli:** Leather pearls made of lambskin-covered glass beads. These are one of your stylist's favorite statement pieces to mix with her old faux opera-length pearls.

Links

"We can all thank British Victorian ladies for first inspiring fashion's passion for wearing lots of links—strands and strands of silver chains in varying lengths; watch chains wrapped at the wrist; links adorned with sentimental charms and lockets," says Melody Rodgers. "Large, small, square, or round links mix with anything and elevate any look. They never date," she adds.

tip Mix your metals. Gold and silver look great jumbled together, but always choose the predominant metal color to complement your skin tone—warm or cool. In general, midlife skin sings next to gold with accents of silver.

Suggested designers:

- Carolee
- Carolee Luxe
- Chanel
- Kara by Kara Ross
- Kenneth Jay Lane
- Lanvin
- Larkspur & Hawk
- Lee Angel
- Mawi
- Philippe Audibert
- Roberto Cavalli Jewelry

Nature

Since the ancients, jewelrymakers have created adornments inspired by what they saw around them: flowers, plants, birds, insects, reptiles, jungle animals, sea creatures, sun, moon, and stars, rendered in materials like metal, wood, ivory, coral, gemstones, you name it. In general, nature themes work best in a few ways: chic but a little comic, or a bit menacing like snarling jungle cats, coiled anacondas, open-mouthed alligators. Wear these plants, critters, and celestials boldly scaled and in all kinds of materials.

Suggested designers:

- Bijoux Heart
- Chanel
- Gerard Yosca
- Jill Alberts
- Kara by Kara Ross
- Kenneth Jay Lane
- Mesi Jilly
- Miriam Haskell
- Roberto Cavalli Jewlery
- Russell Jones
- Ted Rossi

Mixed Media

The recipe: Take one part estate jewelry (inspired by the likes of Harry Winston, Jean Schlumberger, and Verdura) interpreted in brass, glass beads, Swarovski crystals, and semiprecious stones, and combine with one part high-fashion chains, links, and geometric shapes; toss and garnish with found materials like satin ribbon, netting, leather, or vintage charms and you have the magpie mix effect of the mixed media statement piece. Lanvin's jewelry, in particular, launched this wave.

Suggested designers:

- Balenciaga
- Bijoux Heart
- Chanel
- Erickson Beamon
- Janis by Janis Savitt
- Karry'O
- Lanvin
- Ligia Dias
- Louis Vuitton
- Missoni
- Subversive by Justin Giunta
- Tom Binns
- Vera Wang

Antiquity

Early Islamic hammered metals, Greco-Roman coins and snakes, jeweled Byzantine crosses, Mogul Indian luxury combining pearls, rubies, and emeralds, medieval heraldic crests, the Maltese Cross, Renaissance beads and enamels: The look of well-done "appropriated" antiquity is pure style and transcends any trends in any year. Modern looks combined with ancient references or faithful recreations of museum pieces are mixable and stand-alone important. The look is as ageless and timeless as it gets. Always right: pieces created by Kenneth Jay Lane. He's interpreted all of the above and then some. Mr. Lane is the undisputed King of Costume for more than forty years; any category you can think of leads to a Kenneth Jay Lane collection. Affordable, beautifully made high style.

More suggested designers:

- Anne Bezamat
- Ben Amun
- Elizabeth Cole
- Hervé Van der Straeten
- Isharya
- José & Maria Barrera
- Melody Rodgers Collection
- Patrice
- R. J. Graziano
- Roberto Cavalli Jewelry
- Sheila Fajl
- Siman Tu
- Tejani
- Yves St. Laurent Jewelry

Global

The world grows smaller with each fashion season. Global style is the perfect mash-up of everything from tribal, Asian, Middle Eastern, and Indian interpreted with a modern eye. With all things authentic on the wane, indigenous treasures found in markets and bazaars are true luxury goods.

Suggested designers:

- Amrita Singh
- Bounkit
- Isharya
- Kenneth Jay Lane
- Little Gems
- Lizzie Fortunato
- Mawi
- Siman Tu
- SURevolution
- Tejani
- Tuleste Market
- Vivre Collection

Plastic, Resin, Lucite, Acrylic

Organic, sculptural, clean, and easy to combine rings and cuffs in particular are a complement to any style. These should be good quality. Very cheap plastic looks it. Themes like chalk white, black and white, clear, and the simulation of outlawed natural materials like coral, ivory, and tortoiseshell are chic looking and affordable rendered in good-quality plastic, resin, or lucite.

On the vintage front, Bakelite is the original plastic and tagged "the material of a thousand uses." And it was, literally. When it wasn't used for making telephones or bomb casings, celluloid could be dyed to imitate jet, bone, ivory, jade; sometimes inlaid with rhinestones or carved to look like tribal masks or expensive art deco designs. The original Bakelite look inspires many of the best-looking plastic fakes today. "Bakelite colors are rich and distinctive. Chinese red, black and ivory, amber and jade green have a winter 'dressed' look, whereas the sun yellow, grass green, and tomato reds are the perfect look for resort and summer clothes," advises Melody Rodgers.

Suggested designers:

- Alexis Bittar
- Angela Caputi
- Chanel
- Dinosaur Designs
- Fendi
- Jessica Kagan Cushman

- Luc Kieffer
- Marni
- Monies
- Patricia von Musulin
- Pono by Joan Goodman
- Vivre Collection

Web sites for all the jewelry categories above:

- Annebezamat.com
- Barneys.com
- Ben-amun.com
- Bergdorfgoodman.com
- Carolee.com
- Henribendel.com
- Isharya.com
- Jillalberts.com
- Kararossny.com
- Like.com
- Lizziefortunatojewels.com
- Marni.com
- Melodyrodgers.com: Although known as one of the country's finest dealers and experts in estate and vintage gems, Rodgers has developed an affordable costume line inspired by pieces from her collection.
- Neimanmarcus.com
- Net-a-porter.com
- Russelljonesjewelry.com
- Tejani.com
- Vivre.com
- Yoox.com

A Thought or Two About Watches

When the scale of your jewelry grows larger, so should the scale of your watch. Go for a men's watch or a women's style with a larger face. The best complement to bold and unique jewelry is a very simple white face with an unadorned bezel. Gold, silver, or a simple leather band with clean-as-a-whistle looks. This needn't be a bank account draining timepiece. Your stylist loves the dependability and reverse snob appeal of the great-looking styles she finds from Timex, Swatch, Ike, and Nixon to name a few.

- Bloomingdales.com
- Nixonnow.com
- Swatch.com
- Timex.com
- Vivre.com

big BAG theory

Okay, a new handbag is not quite as singular as the explosion that formed the universe, but the creation of the seasonal It Bag has proved to be fashion's Big Bang.

You can't swing last season's hot bag without hitting yet another brand-new designer handbag line. Or twenty. Every designer wants a line of bags (perhaps with a big fat logo front and center) in the hopes that theirs will be the next supernova, the newest trophy bag that every woman will decide she must carry. Casting a steely eye on the landscape of the average department store bag department, I must state clearly that your stylist thinks there are too many damn handbags out there and so few of them truly look good.

Finding a bag that cues cool and confidence is no different than choosing the right shapes for your silhouette. A well-designed bag should have great bones, a defined shape enhanced by color, an interesting surface, and limited and well-placed hardware (if any). The details should all add up to something that is aesthetically balanced and, of course, proportionate for you.

String Theory

In bagland this equals straps, buckles, snaps, zippers, dangling charms, more zippers, fringe, studs—if a handbag is a dog, the best way to disguise its lack of line is to throw on a lot of stuff. The look is a bit indecisive to be hip and ageless. Bags with tat overload are designed for millennials.

The Bags to Add or Update Now

The Distinctive Everyday Bag: If you've always swallowed hard when you've invested in a big bag and opted for the practicality of only black, brown, or saddle, it's time to embrace color. With something rich or bright; a chic dove gray or pale taupe, an exotic skin (real or stamped leather), a slick patent leather, strong but spare looking hardware.

Clutch

Tote Bag

The Quick-Change-at-the-Office Clutch: The bag that shifts your look from workday to drinks. A distinctive-looking leather envelope to tuck under your arm.

A Little Novelty: Animal-printed calf hair, an abstract floral, ethnic prints, beading, embroidery. This is the bag to carry on holiday and weekends. It's a style that expresses your sense of whimsy and the side of your personality you don't wear to the office.

The Exotic Evening Bag: We all have a trim satin evening clutch or two in our stash of reliable bags. Go for the unpredictable appeal of colorful snakeskin, a lavish combination of colors and feathers, dark wood encrusted with glass beads or coral, faux ivory, or a leopard print.

The Much-Improved Tote Bag: It may haul paperwork and a quart of milk home most nights, but it should look great. Trade that grass-stained and road-weary boat tote for a richly colored or metallic nylon or leather, colored water snake, or patent leather. Look for a bag made of lightweight materials to avoid an unbearably heavy bag when it is loaded to the limit.

Stratospheric—Luxury Bags

No one need alert the media. It is well documented that the cost of a luxury bag can equal your monthly mortgage. So invest in or crib the look of the following designers—for day and evening—whose bags have the proportions and details that bring all the elements together in a sophisticated way. As always, study the details at the top.

- **Balenciaga:** Tough chic, perfectly proportioned.
- **Bottega Veneta:** Woven leathers, sublime understatement.

- **Chanel:** Especially the forever chic 2/1955.
- **Devi Kroell:** Exotic skins and materials, shapes.
- **Fendi:** The Selleria bags are classics.
- **Hermès:** Any bag from the House of Hermès will do, thanks very much.
- **Katherine Fleming:** Understated luxe, mixed leathers, subtly embellished.
- **Lanvin:** The Kentucky bag is a neoclassic.
- **Louis Vuitton:** While there is a bag a minute from LVMH, go for a classic shape like the Speedy.
- **Marni:** Minimal and sculptural looks.
- **Mulberry:** The Bayswater is a neoclassic.
- **Pierre Hardy:** Snappy leather satchels with piping.
- **Prada:** One of the best and biggest ranges in bagland.
- **Valextra:** Luxury for the minimalist.
- **Yves St. Laurent:** Gold stars for clean and elegant designs.

> tip Shop at online auction sites like Portero.com for a crack at the preowned luxury bag of your dreams. Ideeli.com sends you alerts via text and e-mail when it's time to bid on your favorites from their selection of brand-new at discounted prices.

Cosmic—Midpriced Bags

This is an oversaturated market. Many of the bags you'll see fall into the contemporary category (which can mean very gobbed-up). Good lines to investigate:

The Establishment

- **Anja Hindmarch**
- **Barneys Private Label**
- **Coach:** Shop for the simplest lines, low on details; skip the Heritage fabric.
- **Cole Haan:** Great woven textures.
- **Dooney & Bourke:** Avoid the Vuitton/Murakami interpretations.
- **Furla**
- **Kate Spade**
- **Miu Miu**

Newer Names

- Alexis Hudson
- Beirn
- Bulga
- Elie Tahari
- Foley & Corina
- Glorinha Paranaguá
- Gryson
- Kotur
- R & Y Augousti
- Stephane Verdino

Cometic—Good Buys

- Club Monaco
- Elliott Lucca
- **Hayden-Harnett:** Their convertible flight tote.
- Linea Pelle
- Maxx New York
- Melie Bianco
- Michael Michael Kors
- M Z Wallace
- Via Spiga

Celestial—Evening Bags (all prices)

- Anja Hindmarch
- Barneys Private Label
- **Clara Kasavina:** Very special colorful skins, intricate metalwork, feathers.
- **Devi Kroell:** Exotic skins, swarovski crystal accents.
- **Jamin Puech:** Rich hippie deluxe.
- Max Azria
- R&Y Augousti
- Stuart Weitzman

Suggested Web sites for all bags:

- Activeendeavors.com
- Barneys.com
- Bergdorfgoodman.com
- Eluxury.com
- Neimanmarcus.com
- Piperlime.com
- Vivre.com

shoes

You've undoubtedly noticed the rather extreme proportions of current shoes. Models trucking down the runway in platforms resembling fetish wear. Sexy shoes suited for the red carpet and carpeted stages with metal poles. Tough-looking sandals made of straps, buckles, grommets, and a few more straps: footwear suited for an urban militia or a remake of *Spartacus*.

For some time now, fashion has dictated that shoes must come in one of two heights: pancake-flat or skyscraping. The popularity of the ballet flat, for example, is no mystery. It has the élan of the original Chanel ballet flat, a "forever ingénue" quality that speaks to the inner Bardot in every woman. The four- and five-inch "Big Foot" statement shoe, however, is fashion's latest antidote to clothing that is more covered up and sophisticated. There is a twisted logic here that you can use to your advantage.

In every stylish, grown-up woman's outfit there should be a point-counterpoint relationship between clothing and accessories. Point: the simple and streamlined-looking clothes we should wear now. Counterpoint: the one or two important-looking accessories that punctuate an outfit. A shoe with presence is a good thing. It is a certain way to make otherwise modern classic clothes look hip. What we are after is how one splits the difference between the avant-garde "orthotic" looks and the soft-porn intimations of a 6-inch stiletto for daytime to find chic and wearable shoe styles.

If you love high heels, the miraculous leg-lengthening sex appeal of heels, the power of a shoe that is so completely female, then you will be loath to abandon them simply because they hurt. While it's true that we all have different thresholds for pain—some women positively glide in 4-inch stilettos while others can barely manage a 2-inch heel without wobbling—for most of us the limit is somewhere between 2½ and 3½ inches, with most of us standing firmly in 2½ inches. According to the American Podiatric Medical Association, the difference between a 2-inch and a 3-inch heel is that the upward shift puts *seven* times the pressure on the ball of the foot. Burning balls. We all know that sensation.

Here are some facts. Our feet have changed by middle age. Most of us now wear a full size larger than we did in our 20s or pre-children. The balls and heels of our feet hurt more now in high heels because by midlife we have lost a significant amount of natural fatty padding. Add in a grab bag of corns, bunions, and shoes that don't fit perfectly or are not well constructed, and a woman is on her knees in no time at all. So let's have a look at shoes that are sexy, gutsy, and still look appropriate for the boardroom (or any room) and not a bordello.

Our initial research leads us to Manolo Blahnik, the eternal master of capturing seasonal now without abandoning all sense of reason. One of the secrets of the enduring love affair women have with Blahnik is that styles are offered in a range of heel heights, from kitten heels to nose bleed and in heel shapes that don't change dramatically from year to year. Mr. Blahnik takes in the news and does his own thing entirely.

Let's also look through Prada, Christian Louboutin, and Jimmy Choo. While the immediate image of a Louboutin heel, for example, is sexed-up and ultra-high (which is to say French), there is a range of sane choices to be found here as well. Since baby boomers are a group who can afford good shoes and are also less likely candidates for vertiginous dagger heels, these designers all include lower heels in a range of smart styles—to be certain to reach us.

For sophisticated women, these lines are the best place to shop for ideas that mix trends awareness with an elegance that is right on the money. And yes, it takes a lot of money to buy a pair of shoes from any of these collections, so if the cost per pair is prohibitive, crib the look from any of these lines in any season. The pumps, sling-backs, and T-strap styles (and who doesn't need one or all of these in her wardrobe?) at Blahnik in particular remain constant from season to season (and are knocked off in all kinds of places, including stores as accessible as Nine West and J.Crew to name a few).

Have a look at Michael Kors—his look always speaks to chic reality. Roger Vivier's distinctive lower chunk heels and pilgrim buckles (the very shoe Catherine Deneuve wore in the film *Belle de Jour*) have a fashion cognoscenti look and influence all kinds of appropriations (Tory Burch for one) at lower prices. Bally and Ferragamo (both lately rejuvenated by new design) and Cassadei are also good bets. Alongside the editorial attention-getters there are always more earthbound options—the looks to buy or to copy at a lower price.

trying on heels

When you try on heels, never settle for the view in the floor-level mirrors. Have a look at yourself in a full-length mirror. You should appear balanced in the shoe. You want a shoe with presence, but not one that dominates (makes your foot look bigger than it is) or that disappears (makes you appear bigger than you are or balanced on two tiny points). Then walk. A lot. Walk the length of the shoe department or store until you are certain that the shoe is comfortable. Walk off the carpeting onto a hard floor if possible. Keep in mind that the full weight of your body should be distributed equally across the length of the shoe, meaning that the balls of your feet as well as your heels are both engaged in supporting your frame. If you feel pitched forward, then take them off and keep looking; it means that the construction of the shoe is shifting your body weight forward onto the balls of your feet. Walk and stand until you are satisfied that the shoes are winners.

Other considerations:

- Shop for shoes in the afternoon when you've retained a bit of fluid for the most accurate read on comfort and fit.

- Be sure that the heel is wide enough near your arch and heel, which support the most weight.

- The shoe's inner sole should mold and contact the length of your arch.

- If it hurts now, it will hobble you later.

- Never let a salesperson convince you that a shoe needs to be broken in. Furthermore, as you walk and stand and walk some more, don't let a salesperson rush you. I let my face go completely blank as if I have lapsed into a trance while I walk around. Salespeople don't come near me until I brandish my charge card in triumph.

If a hit of trend works for your lifestyle, try that slice of platform for a bit of new with walkable comfort. Slip on that chunkier stacked or wood heel for a serving of now that's sturdy enough to walk in without your heels howling in protest. Experiment with toe shapes to find which of them you can wear without sobbing by noon. There is always a way to capture the essence of what looks current without being held hostage by a pair that has you (or your charge cards) wailing in misery.

Comfort and style do not have to be mutually exclusive (at least some of the time). A number of shoe lines have developed designs that fuse state-of-the-art constructions with style. Here is your stylist's roundup from high heels to sandals:

- ▶ **Aquatalia:** Cushioned inner soles and sturdy rubber bottoms; low heels; great looking patent leather boots that look chic in bad weather.

- ▶ **Birkenstock:** For your stylist there is but one sandal style—the Gizeh—and I have worn it for years. It comes in narrow and wide widths, colored patent leathers, and metallic. Astonishingly sleek for what is technically an orthopedic shoe. I log fourteen-hour days on location in these babies.

- ▶ **Cole Haan:** More great-looking fashion styles each season in their Dress Air Collection. Daytime looks including open toes, pointed toes, sling-backs, wedge heels, high-heeled boots, moccasins, and flats as well as sleek evening styles. All have built-in Nike Air cushioning. Heaven is sneaker comfort that looks stylish.

- ▶ **DKNY:** Isola insoles built into most styles.

- ▶ **Ecco:** Ergonomic styles best suited for walking and errands. They do have a few styles that suggest lady rather than land roving; ballet flats, T-straps, ankle boots, wedge heels, and Mary Janes in black suede can walk to work.

- ▶ **Gentle Souls:** More hippie than hip. They are constructed with a memory foam insole with a conforming flaxseed pouch to cradle the arch. Look for their very cushiony ballet flat in black leather and 2¾-inch wedge heel pump in black or brown suede with a rubber bottom.

- ▶ **Geox:** Ballet flat and moccasin styling with a rubber sole that is microperforated to let foot perspiration move through the waterproof sole. The Stefany ballet flat is a favorite all-day walking shoe of European ladies of a certain age.

- ▶ **Naturalizer and Aerosoles:** Both brands that were once synonymous with buying a one-way ticket to Frumptown. In an update-or-perish fashion world, they have raised their style quotient.

Naturalizer leads the charge with heel designs that pick up on runway trends. Flats are a best bet at Aerosoles, but I've also spotted good-looking wedge-heel boots and summer sandals that looked positively Marni-inspired.

▶ **Prada Sport:** Kitten heels with rubber bottoms; low wedge heel boots and ankle boots. Milanese high style built for speed.

▶ **Stuart Weitzman:** High style and with a layer of latex added to inner soles; Weitzman pumps and sandals are very comfortable.

▶ **Taryn Rose:** Developed by Dr. Rose, an orthopedic surgeon. Their claim to a cult following is an ergonomic "shoe last." The shoe is literally made around the form to create optimum weight distribution across the length of the foot. Are these shoes high fashion? Not exactly, but if you have trouble feet, they are a very good looking and stylish alternative to agony.

▶ **Tod's:** Along with their icon, the much-imitated cushioned driving moccasin, Tod's offers a number of heels that are truly comfortable to walk in for hours.

The Shoes That Every Woman Needs in Her Wardrobe

A Nude Pump: Nothing is more flattering than a nude-colored leather pump with a low vamp for extending the line of your leg down to your foot. Look for leather that complements your skin tone. This is one of the ultimate leg lengthening and slimming illusions. Look for a 2- to 3-inch heel with a clean but current shape. Styles with a semirounded toe usually work well. At those times when very pointed toes are in play, do the best you can.

The Black Pump: With the same style qualities as your nude pump. A long line across the top of your foot created by a low vamp revealing a little toe cleavage is essential to keep a black shoe from looking heavy.

---

tip   As Manolo Blahnik once said: "The secret of toe cleavage is that it is a very important part of the sexuality of a shoe. But you must only show the first two cracks." And according to financial guru Suze Orman, "Toe cleavage is the only cleavage that should be shown at the office."

Nude and Black High-Heeled Sandals: These are the "when all else fails these look great and are comfortable" sandals. They should be sleek and simple with a heel height you can walk and stand in. The styling should be uncomplicated enough to be very versatile. These are the sandals that complete any print skirt or dress in your closet; or any addition of a new bright or pale color along with anything black, white, or a combination of the two. You get the picture: the Everysandal.

The Chic and Functional Tall Boot: A regional consideration, of course, but have a packable pair for travel, in good leather or stretch leather. You want these to be as versatile as possible. If you've ever paid a fortune for an It Boot only to find yourself hobbled by a heel that was too high or a toe box that was too pointed for comfort beyond a half hour, then it's time to invest in a wedge-heel boot. The combination of a low wedge heel and a semirounded toe make for a sophisticated but functional look. You add a little height without throwing off your alignment for serious walking. Try black or brown patent leather (when they are on the scene) for boots that add a shot of right now to just about any skirt or simple dress; wipe away bad weather spots with a shot of Windex.

Another Good Option: Anything resembling an expensive and flat black leather riding boot. A look that never dates and looks good with just about anything but black tie—and some would argue that they work here too.

The Ankle Boot: To combine with a pair of trousers for an unbroken leg line. A sleek and simple toe and a comfortable—walkable—heel height. These should be as dressed up as your lifestyle requires. For the office and after-work versatility, a medium-width stack heel will do and a wedge looks right too.

The Puddle-Jumping Boot: No more dodging slush and rain in leather boots. Designers like Loeffler Randall, Sigerson Morrison, Tory Burch, and Aquatalia, to name but a few, make bad weather look good with stack heels and fitted styles in rubber.

The Foolproof Evening Pump: Most of us buy evening shoes as needed to work with a specific look but have one pair of closed-toe black satin or silk faille shoes that are sexy enough to elevate a pair of good black trousers for a cocktail party after work or to pair with a Le Smoking. This is the shoe that pulls through when a sandal isn't appropriate. Choose the highest heel you can manage to walk in comfortably.

Something Metallic: It is always handy to have either a versatile pump like a d'Orsay and/or sandals with a sleek 2- to 2½-inch heel. A clean style in metallic is one of the best quick-change elements in a wardrobe—instantly elevating simple pieces for day into evening-ready looks. Go for matte over very shiny surfaces.

A Chic Walking Shoe: To take you to the office (where you slip on those high heels) and for weekends and errands. Especially for casual workplaces where flats are an acceptable look all day, have something supportive but stylish. Your stylist implores you to stop wearing your workout sneakers for anything but exercise.

A Non-athletic Sneaker: Go for a classic like slip-in Vans; Jack Purcells; Stan Smiths; simple styles from Puma, Lacoste, and Adidas. These are the walking sneakers that don't destroy an outfit. Wearing workout shoes, especially any big blocky white sneakers with street clothes, adds ten years (at least) to your appearance.

More Ageless Options

Think about adding these to your wardrobe in a low vamp pump, a d'Orsay pump, a T-strap, or a sandal—high or low heeled.

Animal Print: In printed calf hair or cloth to add an instant (and timeless) looking dash of high fashion to an outfit; in all-purpose leopard, of course; zebra for graphic black and white.

Snakeskin: The luxe neutral that works with everything.

tip When you buy anything in snake, make sure that the size of the snake scales are in proportion with the size of the item. Smaller scales are ideal for shoes and sandals. Really walk in snakeskin before making a commitment. If they feel stiff and papery, then pass. The tanning chemicals and any dye used to add color can stiffen the skin. The darker the color of the dye, the harsher it is on the skin. Natural and light-hued skins are generally softest and last the longest.

Two-toned: Chanel-inspired two-toned spectator pump; multi-toned combinations of leather, patent leather, and suede. This is a savvy way to add high style and save money with a shoe that elevates a variety of looks from work clothes to jeans.

Cloth flat in an animal print

High-heeled moccasin

Metallic trim: On a black leather or suede shoe or sandal for a goes-anywhere look day or night.

Cloth: The ideal way to pull in trends in printed satin; linen; brocades; globally inspired ethnic prints like batik, ikat, and Kenyan panel prints; Indian brocades; menswear flannels, metallic washed linens, cotton, or wool lace.

Embellished: Embroideries; beading; novelty trims like raffia or feathers.

And when they are on the scene:

The Shoe Bootie: A feminine way to add a flattering volume at the foot and a little "tough" to an outfit without looking as though you tried too hard.

The High-Heeled Lace-up Oxford or Moccasin: Again, adds a little oomph and ageless cool to an outfit (without dressing like a fashion victim).

shopping suggestions

Shopping for shoes from high-fashion designer lines once you have located your fit and heel height is a no-brainer. They are the expensive statement accent that ups the ante of any outfit you wear them with. But the cost per pair is, of course, très cher. There are plenty of lines that offer good looks for less than stratospheric prices.

Suggested Designers at Bridge and Better Prices

Bridge

- **Coach:** This line is never without the pump, the sandal, the boot that is trends-aware; well made and walkable. Caveat: Skip the Heritage print fabrics.
- **Cole Haan:** Fashion and Nike Air. Yes, please.
- **Delman:** Styles that balance trends and reality.
- **DKNY:** Insolia gel insoles built in for comfort.
- **Kate Spade:** The shoe line improves every season. A range of heels and toe shapes that look like a lot for the money. Spotted recently: a pump best described as a very faithful ode to Christian Louboutin.
- **Kors Michael Kors:** Takes on the trends but in a wearable fashion; classics like moccasins and other flats are always in the mix. They can run large.
- **Loeffler Randall:** Nice shapes, nice materials, very nice fit, nice edge.
- **Sigerson Morrison:** Trends in an understated way. You will never look like a fashion casualty in these shoes.
- **Stuart Weitzman:** Pretty much every style a lady can want for day or night. Thanks, Stuart!
- **Studio Pollini:** Great low-heeled boots.
- **Tahari:** Good looks, and they get better with every season.
- **Tory Burch:** Fantastic shapes; Roger Vivier–inspired lower heels, the Reva flat; chunky wood heel pumps but you must love her logo.

Better-to-Good Buys

- **Anne Klein**
- **Enzo Angiolini:** Modern classics.
- **J.Crew:** Refined yet cheeky classics with heels lower than 4 inches.
- **Lauren Ralph Lauren:** Modern classics.
- **Nine West:** Trendy 4-inch heels side by side with realistic heel heights and practical finds alike; good source for sandals with a look but not a big price tag. Sizes run a full size large and they can be wide.
- **Studio 9:** Nine West's more expensive line of hot off-the-runway looks. They run big. Walk and walk in the store.
- **Via Spiga:** Trends, big time. Well priced and fairly well made.

I Can Walk!

Insoles and insert pads will improve the comfort and fit of your favorite shoes. There are more available for shoe doctoring than you can shake a stick at. I have tried them all—particularly on shoots to give the models a break when the photographer asks for lots of running and jumping in heels. Here is what I use in my kit in descending order:

- **Insolia** (insolia.com): Pageant winner! Gel inserts developed by a podiatrist. They are designed to shift weight from the ball of the foot to the heel, improving body alignment and balance. These work so well that it feels as if you are wearing lower heels. I have the cobbler put Isolia inserts into anything with a heel.
- **Grippy Steps from Apara:** Runner-up. Stays-in-place comfort.
- **Airplus Love My Straps:** Second Runner-up. Padded strap liners . . . oh! much better!!
- **Foot Petals:** Miss Congeniality. The insole liners (lavender scented, no less) provide less cushioning and tend to tear easily. Expensive for short-lived quality.
- **Dr. Scholl's:** Group Hug. A wide assortment of ball pads and heel pads. It takes fooling around with different combinations.

Web sites for all shoes:

- **Barneys.com**
- **Bergdorfgoodman.com**
- **Eluxury.com**
- **Neimanmarcus.com**
- **Nordstrom.com**
- **Piperlime.com:** Well edited.
- **Saks.com**
- **Shoebuy.com**
- **Shoes.com**
- **Zappos.com**

Shoes of Surrender

One final footwear-related thought before we move on. There are certain shoes—besides big chunky fitness shoes—that should not be worn with street clothes. That in fact should never be worn outside of your kitchen, garden, a hiking trail, runs to the town dump. These are Crocs and Merrells. I know they are comfortable. I understand that your feet cry out for them when they are apart. But ladies, nothing transmits "I have given up on myself completely" like a colorful (did I mention goofy?) pair of Crocs or a chunky Merrell mule or Mary Jane (or whatever style). Please. I am begging you. Just. Don't.

eyeglasses

Talk about split-second impressions. Your eyeglasses are an instant read on your style IQ. If you need glasses, wear great-looking glasses. Your eyeglasses are no different from any other fashion accessory in your wardrobe. Wear what looks flattering and au courant and what telegraphs that you pay attention to fashion.

Of course, finding just the right pair requires experimentation, but to avoid flying blind when you walk into an eyewear store, Rene Soltis, optician and spokesperson for the Vision Council, breaks down the process:

The Rules

"Match the scale of a frame with your facial proportions," advises Soltis. Naturally, delicate features are overwhelmed by big and thick frames (as is a petite silhouette overall; think the Olsen twins and their oversized shades). Teeny frames will naturally look out of place on a full face; taller and voluptuous girls can combine flattering shape with larger-scale frames.

"Contrast—rather than mirror—the shape of a frame to the shape of your face," she advises. If you've never been quite sure of the shape, then look at your face fresh from the shower. Slick your hair back and have a look in the mirror. "When in doubt, stick to some very simple basics: If you have a curved or full face, avoid round frames and try angular styles. Conversely, if your face is more angular, go with styles that are rounded and have curves."

Facial Shapes

A **round face** is essentially the same length and width with full cheeks and subtle, if any, angles.

- Choose slightly angular frames to narrow the appearance of your face.
- Choose high or midheight temples to create the look of a longer profile.
- Pass on very rounded or square styles that exaggerate facial fullness.
- Pass on frames that are deeper (longer) on your face (or they'll rest flush on your cheeks) than they are wide.

Good Bets

- **For eyeglasses:** Narrow, rectangular shapes; angled corners; square shapes.
- **For sunglasses:** Larger rectangles with subtly upturned corners draw the focus upward and out to deemphasize full cheeks.

A **square face** has a structure defined by a strong jawline and broad cheekbones; your face is as long as it is wide.

- Choose gently curved, narrow styles to minimize a square shape and to subtly lengthen the face.
- Choose frames with weight on the top.
- Pass on frames that are flat on the bottom, as this will exaggerate the square shape.
- Pass on frames that are more vertical than horizontal.

Good Bets

- **For eyeglasses:** Try styles with a strong upper line and a curved bottom to give angular features a rounder appearance; color that complements your eye color and rimless bottoms to draw the focus up and away from a strong jaw and chin.
- **For sunglasses:** Rounded shapes; aviators with soft, rounded edges. Gradient lenses that are dark on the top and lighter at the bottom accomplish the same focus shift upward to the eyes and brow line.

An **oval shape** is as close to symmetrical as it gets. Ovals can wear a variety of shapes. The key is to keep any frame in proportion with the size of your face and features.

- Choose frames that are as wide (or wider) than the broadest part of your face.
- Pass on low or curved temples, which will disrupt the natural balance of your face.

Good Bets

- **For eyeglasses:** Flattering shapes like the rectangle with corners that angle upward, lift the face, draw attention to the eyes, and highlight cheekbones; interesting color—from bold to clear—will further enhance the effect.
- **For sunglasses:** Rectangles, soft squares, and ovals alike can all look flattering; think about skin-tone-flattering color and avoid going too oversized for the size of your proportions.

A **heart-shaped face** is broadest at the forehead and cheekbones and tapers to a narrow chin:

- Choose frame shapes like rectangles to balance the difference in the width between your forehead and chin.
- Choose frames that are slightly wider at the bottom to add the illusion of width in your lower face.
- Choose low temples to balance your facial proportions.
- Pass on frames that have a strong line at the brow or that have bold or dark color that adds weight to the top of the frame.

Good Bets

- **For eyeglasses:** Semi-rimless and rimless styles will open up your face and balance the proportions; lenses that are slightly wider across the bottom also balance the symmetry by adding depth to the lower half of your face.
- **For sunglasses:** Frames that complement your skin tone create a balanced and low-contrast appearance. Choose solid-colored rather than gradient lenses that have depth at the top and are lighter at the bottom.

For All Shapes

"Be sure that your eyes are centered in the glasses for the best fit and optimized vision. Choose antireflective lenses for all your eyeglasses and the strongest UV protection for sunglass lenses. If you spend a lot of time in front of a computer screen, ask for lenses that will reduce computer vision syndrome and eliminate glare and eyestrain," advises Rene Soltis.

Balance Eyeglasses with Eyebrows

Regardless of your facial shape, take the natural shape and arch of your brow line into consideration to find the most flattering frames. "You don't want to create the appearance of a double brow, so choose a frame shape that mirrors the arch of your eyebrows. Having your brow peek over the top gives you an eternally surprised expression. If the brow peeks out under the frame, in the middle of the lens, it gives you the appearance of a permanent scowl! The only exception is for sunglasses, which can be oversized and tend to cover the brow completely . . . don't worry, the dark lenses will camo the scowl look," says Soltis.

Color Codes

"Don't confine your choice to only neutral colors for your eyewear. Go for flattering instead. The idea now is to choose what brings warmth and color to your face. Opt for plastic rather than metal frames, which can look very draining on older skin. The best options will complement (not match) your eye color and your skin tone—warm or cool—so choose new frames as you would a flattering new top, for example. Don't be afraid to choose a definitive color. Just be sure to avoid a strong color contrast between the frame and your skin. The effect will look severe, and that is visually aging," Soltis adds.

It's vital to complement your hair color as well. The overall effect should be an eye-pleasing and harmonious color statement.

Suggestions for:

- **Brown hair:** Try deep, rich browns, wine or burgundy, amber tortoise.
- **Black hair:** Avoid any frames with yellow or a yellow cast. Try black, blue/black combination, tortoise or dark brown and gray, deep gunmetal.
- **Red hair:** If your skin is very fair, try translucent with a beige cast; browns with pink or coral undertones.
- **Golden blond hair:** Think earth tones. Medium browns with undertones of yellow, olive, amber, or rose. Translucent frames can also create a striking, skin-flattering effect.

Black frames look best on platinum or ashy blonds with darker, strong brows and brown eyes.

- **Gray hair:** Avoid yellow undertones. Instead bring color to your face with red, wine and burgundy, navy, or jewel tone tones. Experiment with blues and greens. Avoid shiny metals.

Illusions

Rene Soltis recommends these optical illusions:

- A clear bridge widens the appearance of close-set eyes.
- A dark bridge narrows the appearance of very wide-set eyes. Try frames that have a bridge bar that is thicker and more prominent to achieve a narrowing effect.
- Contrasting temples will widen the appearance of a narrow face.
- Temples that rest low on a frame shorten the appearance of a long profile, as do inverted temples, which are placed at the bottom of the lens area.
- High temples, or end pieces, placed at the top of the lens area lengthen the appearance of a short and round face.

Shopping Suggestions for Eyewear

Lenscrafters, Pearle Vision, Sunglass Hut, and Solstice Sunglass stores are all owned by Safilo, the same Italian eyewear conglomerate that produces styles for many big-name designers including Dior, Armani, Gucci, Ralph Lauren, and Yves St. Laurent, among many. The other big player in eyewear is Luxottica, which produces frames for Prada, Chanel, and Persol among many, owns Ilori, the upmarket eyewear chain.

Good news for shoppers everywhere: What you find in one store you will find in all of their stores—no matter where you live. This is also good news for saving money. Since you do not have to buy your frames where you have your prescription filled, try things on and gather style numbers at the big stores and then track your frames down (or last season's very similar model) online for less.

If you prefer a hip, less logo'd and seen-everywhere look, ask for glasses by Modo and their designer stable of Fabien Baron, Derek Lam, and 3.1 Philip Lim at specialty eyewear boutiques.

Optometrist Selima Salaun designs one of the very best ranges of eyeglasses out there. Her Selima Optique stores in New York City, L.A., and Paris offer her unique and ultracool take on everything from the classics to Euro racy looks in eyewear and sunglasses. Unadorned and in a sophisticated range of colors, these are frames you won't see coming and going. You won't find a frameless titanium style in the lot. Her glasses can be found at selimaoptique.com. If you love the look and price of vintage frames as much as your stylist does, here are two of my favorite New York eyewear haunts and their shopping Web sites. Fabulous Fanny's (fabulousfannys.com) is an East Village institution offering an incredible selection of vintage frames from the '60s, '70s, and '80s (and earlier if you'd like). There is always something satisfying in finding the original source of a current look. Linda Derector (lindaderector.com) stocks more than six thousand pairs of vintage eyeglasses in her New York City store, and her Web site is filled with great choices.

Readers

If you are currently reading fine print with a pair of ready-to-go prescription glasses from the drugstore (particularly if you wear them at the office or pull them out in public with any frequency), it's time for an upgrade. Good-looking options can be had from eyebobs (eyebobs.com), Corinne McCormick (corinnemccormack.com), and ICU (icueyewear.com).

Discount Web sites:

- **Bestbuyeyeglasses.com**
- **Calabriareaders.com** (readers)
- **Debspecs.com** (readers)
- **Glassesetc.com**
- **Pronto.com**
- **Shopzilla.com**
- **Zappos.com** (sunglasses only)

scarves

The way a woman ties her scarf tells you a lot about her nature. Precisely folded and tied neatly or twisted and wrapped around the neck with abandon? I'm afraid I must trot out the standard image of chic: the French woman in a scarf tied with such insouciance yet authority that you can't help but notice how great she looks. Who cares exactly what she has on? Just look at that damn scarf! I guess for the very same reason that they don't get fat, French women have scarf-tie-chic DNA. But the good news is that the Ageless Woman has learned a few tricks herself. She has a wardrobe of scarves, and she knows how to tie them. She uses scarves to create a stunning focal point here or there and to act as camouflage wherever needed.

Choose your scarves now— in patterns and shades warm or cool—as you choose color cosmetics and hair color. The colors next to your face should do all the magical things we talked about earlier: Boost your skin tone and coax those highlights in your eyes and hair out of hiding. Interesting looking, bulk-free coverage is what our necks require now. Here are a few things to know about the scarves you need now:

Go for color: Your stylist does not subscribe to the old-school dictum that the older your face, the more subtle the color next to it should be. I say go for bold color and gutsy pattern. Personally, I've always considered my scarves a bit of a lipstick substitute when I don't wear it, and don't want to look paler than a washer load of whites.

Choose lightweight: Silks and lightweight weaves like Italian linen or tissue-weight cashmere wrap and drape like a dream. That thickish and scratchy tartan you've worn since grad school is not the right look now.

The Ideal Ageless Scarf Wardrobe

Big Silk Squares: Indulge in a little Vive la Femme whimsy with scarf prints. Every big designer makes scarves à la the classic Hermès status silks. Who cares about the pedigree if the folded result displays enough good color, a patch or two of pattern, and that the exposed ends are nicely finished.

Try a choker style: Fold your square in half to form a triangle. Fold the 90-degree point back into the center and fold over again with the smooth edge until you arrive at a width that flatters the length of your neck. Tie the scarf in a knot at the base of your neck, and turn it around so the ends hang down your back. **Option #1:** Leave the knot in the front. **Option #2:** Tie in an off-center knot. How's that for rocket science?

Long Rectangles: Get your Global on with rectangles in vintage ikat prints, or coarsely woven cotton, linen, silk, or cashmere solids or prints. Go for a metallic woven and don't forget the animal magnetism.

Try the Italian style on the previous page—the name for a rectangle folded once lengthwise, then folded again in half. Place this new four-ply around your neck and pull the loose ends through the loop end. A grade-A face framer and a dandy way to fill in a neckline. Or try the Twizzler—hold the rectangle at each end and lightly twist it up until it resembles a nice long Twizzler (or Red Vine, depending on where you grew up). Begin to wrap the scarf at the center front of your neck, wrap to the back, and bring it back around to the front and tie. Works best with lightweight wovens and rough silks.

Oblongs: A very handy shape to pull out in a fix. The drape of an oblong passes over your midriff and tummy and disguises them with a lengthening vertical line. Have solids and prints on hand.

Try this classic: Worn simply by wrapping the scarf around your neck and letting the ends hang free down your front. More rocket science. Or try it loosely tied in a bow: When bows are in fashion, tie a black silk or silk chiffon oblong into a loose bow that drapes and wear around the neck of a white shirt for a menswear touch. Wear one tied with a jewel-neck sweater in place of a necklace. What makes the look work is soft drape. A bow that is stiff and small, while very high fashion, can look very Madame Secretary on midlife ladies.

always ageless
accessory buys

- Faux opera-length pearls

- A chunky link bracelet or charm bracelet

- Drop earrings for color or evening
  dazzle (that hit your
  cheek, jaw, or neck in a
  flattering place)

- Chunky right-hand
  ring for day and big
  faux cocktail ring

- A classic, unadorned
  men's watch

- A statement necklace in costume
  jewelry: new or vintage

- A chunky cuff (as thick as works for the length of your arm)

- Earring basics: pearl studs, diamond studs, and gold and silver
  hoops—real or good-quality faux

- Chic and skin-flattering eyeglasses and sunglasses

- A great quality, clean-lined handbag for everyday

- A chic clutch in leather; an exotic reptile look, metallic

- An embellished or printed novelty bag

- An unexpected evening bag in leopard, calf hair, snakeskin, feathers

- Scarves: silks in scarf prints, ethnic prints, novelty prints, soft and
  lightweight wovens in square, oblong, and rectangle

- Perfect pumps in nude and black

- Simple unadorned sandals in nude and black: heels and flats

- Flat boots: knee high and ankle

- A metallic shoe: heels and flats

- A printed cloth shoe: heels and flats

- Thin- to medium-width "go with anything" belts in nude, black,
  metallic, leopard, colors

- An exotic, embellished cummerbund or sash belt with a no-
  buckle smooth finish

Wraps: There is always an argument to be made for the pashmina. Lovely colors, soft, warm, easy to carry, but sadly really frumpy when worn around bare shoulders and clutched up in the hand like an over-sized tea towel.

tie tip Tied at your shoulders and folded over once and off center. C'est ça. The simpler the better. You'll get a lot more play from a square shawl of at least 54 inches in tissue-weight wool with exotic looking details, for example. Fold it into a triangle, tie it at your shoulders with an off-center knot, or just flip the ends in different directions: one up and one down.

afterword

The last notion of style evolution I'll leave you with is this: *Ageless* is, finally, the rejection of conformity. What I find most curious about the older women I see every day dressed like their millennial daughters or young coworkers is that they are copying a style that is about the look of the minute. The same look of the minute that all their friends are wearing.

While this is a group that defines itself by its need for individual expression, in reality they are every bit as conformist as every other group of 20-somethings before them. It is the very rare young woman who has yet to figure out a truly individual style. She just hasn't lived enough yet.

Time, experience, and perspective give personal style its seasoning. None of us should hold our breath waiting for fashion's youth obsession to change. Clothing designers will always be inspired by young muses and the edge and energy of youth, but the fashion world is in its current state of flux because of us. There will be more clothing lines designed to capture our spending power. We should always remain curious and selectively inspired by what is new while keeping in mind what works for us. If ever there was a group of women who could reinvent style in midlife and beyond, it's us—more than 45 million of us who can lead by example. And as someone once said, the greatest joy in the world is to begin!

acknowledgments

My thanks and gratitude to my editor Lauren Marino and my agent Tanya McKinnon at Mary Evans Inc.; Anja Kroencke for her inspired illustrations; Susi Oberhelman for her beautiful design; Mary Nelson Sinclair for her tireless research; Melody Rodgers, Melody Rodgers NYC for her storehouse of knowledge; Susan Nethero of {intimacy} stores for sharing her expertise; Rene Soltis at the Vision Council; Ann Magnin, Ann Magnin Public Relations; Libby Bennett, my very groovy mother-in-law, who at eighty-eight still loves clothes; George Bennett, my husband and the best sounding board, line editor, and lingerie consultant a girl could ask for; and Belle, pug and editorial assistant extraordinaire.